# For a Future to Be Possible

## THICH NHAT HANH

PARALLAX PRESS
BERKELEY, CALIFORNIA

Parallax Press
P.O. Box 7355
Berkeley, CA 94707
www.parallax.org

Parallax Press is the publishing division of Unified Buddhist Church, Inc.

Cover design by Graciela Galup.
Text design by Gopa & Ted2, Inc.

Library of Congress Cataloging-in-Publication Data

Nhát Hanh, Thích.
  For a future to be possible / Thich Nhat Hanh.
     p. cm.
  Previously published: 1998.
  ISBN-13: 978-1-888375-66-4
  ISBN-10: 1-888375-66-3
  1. Five Precepts (Buddhism) I. Title.
  BQ5495.F67 2007
  294.3'444--dc22
                            2006102387

1 2 3 4 5 / 11 10 09 08 07

# Contents

# Foreword:
## The Road Is Your Footsteps

JOAN HALIFAX

Wanderer, the road is your
footsteps, nothing else;
wanderer, there is no path,
you lay down a path in walking.

In walking, you lay down a path
and when turning around
you see the road you'll
never step on again.
Wanderer, path there is none,
only tracks on the ocean foam.*

WHENEVER I think about keeping the precepts in the practice of Buddhism, what Thich Nhat Hanh calls the Five Mindfulness Trainings, I think about two qualities: discernment and kindness. The Buddhist vows of good and right conduct, created in the time of the historical Buddha, are tied to the history and culture they come from. When the precepts are brought up to date and made culturally relevant, as in the case of Thich Nhat Hanh's

*"The Road Is Your Footsteps," by Antonio Machado, translated by Francisco Valera.

retranslation and commentary in this book, our Buddhist vows are basically good medicine for our wayward minds and forgetful hearts. They remind us to see and point us toward kindness. Although our Original Nature might well be without blemish, most of us seem to have no small accumulation of "dust" on the mirror of our minds. Practice is about housecleaning. Precepts are a reminder that the house needs to be cleaned, and we best not forget that we forget to take care of ourselves and others. "Here's how," say the precepts.

Practice is also about crafting the art of living beautifully, honestly, and with strength and dignity. Precepts are a refinement of this craft; they are a mindfulness tool and a tool of compassion that can open body, speech, and mind to original wholesomeness. Precepts are also about deepening the experience of community. Thây, as Thich Nhat Hanh is known to his friends and students, has said often that the precepts are our protectors: they protect us and they protect other beings as well.* If we are to live in peace with each other, with the four worlds (mineral, plant, animal, and human) of Grandmother Earth, we need to dedicate ourselves to the path of nonviolence toward all. We see ourselves in each thing, in each being. We know that harming others through body, speech, or mind is harming a part of ourselves. We see that our so-called individual identity is tied to all other identities, and so we are not a separate or local self, but in a continuum with all else. Thus the precepts can bring us to this sense of deep responsibility toward the greater world and also responsibility for ourselves as well. They are, in essence, a way for us to take care of our global and very local community.

---

* Thây is a Vietnamese word meaning "teacher."

Yet the precepts also have their shadow. Like any guidelines, taken too rigidly, they can breed piety, self-righteousness, humorlessness, and even vengeance justified as "helpful criticism." I have seen the precepts used as a weapon against others instead of as a tool of understanding. The humiliation and punishment of those who break the precepts seems to me to be counter to a Buddhist view of seeing ourselves as not separate from others and as empty of any identity. There are saner means for creating understanding in those who are deluded or in the thrall of aggression or passion. The way to understanding is through understanding, to paraphrase Thich Nhat Hanh. How can we help a heart to stop defending itself? How can our Original Innocence be retrieved? Certainly not through the coercion of punishment and public humiliation. This has been a big and sticky question in the West. I believe we have not yet seen our way through to a solution of compassion for all. Suffering has many faces. Victim and tyrant both suffer. Alienation takes many forms, including greed, jealousy, sexual obsession, righteousness, anger, hatred, hypocrisy, and other forms of acute confusion. Suffering's face is abuser and abused.

It is also too often true that people hide behind the precepts and practice in secret the opposite of what they preach. Yet the fact is that we break precepts all the time. If we are able to see this, then there is some small possibility that we may cultivate compassion not only for our very human selves but for others as well. The Japanese have an expression that seems to capture the sense of pathos that is at the heart of our all too human dilemma: *mono no aware*, "the slender sadness." Simply by living we take life. Leather shoes and belts, breathing in and out, a cup of water, a flushing toilet, a stroll in the forest, raising mustard greens, flying here and there, the daily newspaper: in each, a thousand things are dying and being born. Our thoughts can never be as pure as white snow in a silver bowl. Our speech is only so skillful. Treating our bodies and the bodies of others as precious stuff is not so easy, driven as we are by duty or desire, fear or confusion. We are called to be honest about the struggle most of us face daily in living a wholesome life. Our world is not in a very healthy state. Between the degradation of our environment, the loss of values and meaning on a global and local level and the plain stuff of human suffering, the odds are pretty much against one realizing much long-lasting joy or equanimity. And this is why we practice: enlightenment is an accident; practice makes one accident-prone.

I believe that it is through our failures that the muscles of truth, compassion, and courage strengthen. Where we have been weak is where we find strategies for the development of our strengths. And often it takes a thorn to remove a thorn. Sometimes an act of so-called non-virtue is a helpful and skillful means. Striving for an unrealistic and exaggerated perfection is a madness that produces inauthenticity; in effect it can forge a monster of pretentiousness. Fall down into the darkness. Where are the knees of humility touching? Practice standing up. The spines of ten thousand things rise up with you. We are not alone in this wonderful struggle for truth. Thây once wrote that it is through our lives that we experiment with truth. The precepts are not truth. They usually point to the kindest alternative. But when a monk or nun in Vietnam offers the living body to the fire, where stands the truth of non-harming?

Once, in the highlands of Nepal at Thupten Chöling Monastery near Junbese in the Solu Valley, hundreds of monks and nuns sat patiently in the *gompa* courtyard as the doctor with us gave them medical attention. Many were suffering from tuberculosis and cancer. All were smiling; self-pity was not present. We Westerners could hardly bear the sight of so much pain experienced with such great equanimity. When standing in their midst, I remembered the image of the first Vietnamese monk who immolated himself. His body in flames, he sat still in his own inferno, a "lotus in a sea of fire." Was it the precepts that brought him to this radical act of self-annihilation? In part, I believe that the precepts protected him as he gave his flesh to the flames. In taking his own life, he knew he might save many. And it takes keen and radical discernment as well as great love to make such an offering to others. Breaking the precepts, he kept the precepts.

What then can we do with the precepts? How can we live through them in a nondual manner? What must be done to retrieve Original Innocence, our natural virtue? I don't believe it is by putting on something that isn't who we are. Wearing feathers does not make us a flying bird. The poet Antonio Machado reminds us that we lay down the road in the walking. As he was dying, the Buddha told his friends that they were to question teachers and teachings. Take nothing on faith. Study the self, said Dogen. Cultivate discernment. Truth is to be found where one's foot is. Can we look deeply and see the universe in the dust beneath our feet? Penetrate the present moment sharply. And relax. "Use the precepts as a mirror," Thich Nhat Hanh says. Let the precepts be our ally, not our master. And know that the great question for most of us still remains unanswered.

# Introduction

I HAVE BEEN in the West for over forty years and for much of that time I've led mindfulness retreats in Europe, Australia, and North America. During these retreats, I hear many stories of suffering. Much of this suffering is the result of physical, verbal, and emotional violence, alcoholism, drug abuse, and sexual abuse that has been passed down from generation to generation.

There is a deep malaise in society. When we put a young person in this society without trying to protect him, he receives violence, hatred, fear, and insecurity every day, and eventually he gets sick. Our conversations, TV programs, advertisements, newspapers, and magazines all water the seeds of suffering in young people, and in not-so-young people as well. We feel a kind of vacuum in ourselves, and we try to fill it by eating, reading, talking, smoking, drinking, watching TV, going to the movies, or even overworking. Taking refuge in these things only makes us feel hungrier and less satisfied, and we want to ingest even more. We need some guidelines, some preventive medicine, to protect ourselves, so we can become healthy again. We have to find a cure for our illness. We have to find something that is good, beautiful, and true in which we can take refuge.

When we drive a car, we are expected to observe certain rules so that we do not have an accident. Two thousand five hundred years ago, the Buddha offered certain guidelines, called the Five Wonderful Precepts, to his lay students to help them live peaceful, wholesome, and happy lives. Precepts are different from "commandments" and "rules." They are the insights born from mindful observation and direct experience of suffering. They are the guidelines that help us train ourselves to live in a way that protects us and those around us. As we continue the training, our understanding and practice of the precepts deepen. No one can be perfect when he or she just begins the training, and even during the time of training.

I have translated these precepts for modern times as the Five Mindfulness Trainings because mindfulness is at the foundation of each one of them. With mindfulness, we are aware of what is going on in our bodies, our feelings, our minds, and the world, and we avoid doing harm to ourselves and others. Mindfulness protects us, our families, and our society, and ensures a safe and happy present and a safe and happy future. Precepts are the most concrete expression of the practice of mindfulness.

In Buddhism, mindfulness, concentration, and insight always go together. It is impossible to speak of one without the other two. This is called the Threefold Training: *sila*, the practice of the mindfulness trainings; *samadhi*, the practice of concentration; and *prajña*, the practice of insight. Mindfulness trainings, concentration, and insight exist in a way that is interconnected. They inter-are. Practicing the mindfulness trainings brings about concentration, and concentration is needed for insight. Mindfulness is the ground for concentration, concentration allows us to look deeply, and insight is the fruit of looking deeply. When we are mindful, we can see that by refraining from doing *this*, we prevent *that* from happening. We arrive at our own unique insight, not something imposed on us by an outside authority. It is the fruit of our own observation. Practicing the mindfulness trainings, therefore, helps us be more calm and concentrated and brings more insight and enlightenment, which makes our practice of the mindfulness trainings more solid. The three are intertwined; each helps the other two, and all three bring us closer to final liberation. They prevent us from falling back into illusion and suffering. When we are able to step out of the stream of suffering, it is called *anasvara* in Sanskrit, "to stop leaking." As long as we continue to leak, we are like a vessel with a crack, and inevitably we will fall into suffering, sorrow, and delusion.

The Five Mindfulness Trainings are love itself. To love is to understand, protect, and bring well-being to the object of our love. The practice of the trainings accomplishes this. We protect ourselves and each other and we obtain even deeper peace and joy.

What is the best way to practice the mindfulness trainings? I do not know. I am still learning, along with you. I appreciate the phrase that is used in the Five Mindfulness Trainings: to "learn ways." We don't know everything. But we can minimize our ignorance. Confucius said, "To know that you don't know is the beginning of knowing." I think this is the way to practice. We should be modest and open so we can learn together. We need a Sangha, a community, to support us, and we need to stay in close touch with our society to practice the mindfulness trainings well. Many of today's problems did not exist at the time of the Buddha. Therefore, we have to look deeply together in order to develop the insights that will help us and our children find better ways to live wholesome, happy, and healthy lives.

Do you care about yourself? Do you care about me? Do you care about life? Do you care about the Earth? The best way to answer these questions is to practice the Five Mindfulness Trainings. In that way, you teach with your actions and not just with words. If you really care, please practice these mindfulness trainings for your own protection and for the protection of other people and species. If we do our best to practice, a future will be possible for us, our children, and our children's children.

—Thich Nhat Hanh

# The Five Mindfulness Trainings

## FIRST MINDFULNESS TRAINING

AWARE OF the suffering caused by the destruction of life, I am committed to cultivating compassion and learning ways to protect the lives of people, animals, plants, and minerals. I am determined not to kill, not to let others kill, and not to condone any act of killing in the world, in my thinking, and in my way of life.

## SECOND MINDFULNESS TRAINING

Aware of the suffering caused by exploitation, social injustice, stealing, and oppression, I am committed to cultivating loving kindness and learning ways to work for the well-being of people, animals, plants, and minerals. I will practice generosity by sharing my time, energy, and material resources with those who are in real need. I am determined not to steal and not to possess anything that should belong to others. I will respect the property of others, but I will prevent others from profiting from human suffering or the suffering of other species on Earth.

## THIRD MINDFULNESS TRAINING

Aware of the suffering caused by sexual misconduct, I am committed to cultivating responsibility and learning ways to protect the safety and integrity of individuals, couples, families, and society. I am determined not to engage in sexual relations without love and a long-term commitment. To preserve the happiness of myself and others, I am determined to respect my commitments and the commitments of others. I will do everything in my power to protect children from sexual abuse and to prevent couples and families from being broken by sexual misconduct.

## FOURTH MINDFULNESS TRAINING

Aware of the suffering caused by unmindful speech and the inability to listen to others, I am committed to cultivating loving speech and deep listening in order to bring joy and happiness to others and relieve others of their suffering. Knowing that words can create happiness or suffering, I am determined to speak truthfully, with words that inspire self-confidence, joy, and hope. I will not spread news that I do not know to be certain and will not criticize or condemn things of which I am not sure. I will refrain from uttering words that can cause division or discord, or that can cause the family or the community to break. I am determined to make all efforts to reconcile and resolve all conflicts, however small.

## FIFTH MINDFULNESS TRAINING

Aware of the suffering caused by unmindful consumption, I am committed to cultivating good health, both physical and mental, for myself, my family, and my society by practicing mindful eating, drinking, and consuming. I will ingest only items that preserve peace, well-being, and joy in my body, in my consciousness, and in the collective body and consciousness of my family and society. I am determined not to use alcohol or any other intoxicant or to ingest foods or other items that contain toxins, such as certain TV programs, magazines, books, films, and conversations. I am aware that to damage my body or my consciousness with these poisons is to betray my ancestors, my parents, my society, and future generations. I will work to transform violence, fear, anger, and confusion in myself and in society by practicing a diet for myself and for society. I understand that a proper diet is crucial for self-transformation and for the transformation of society.

# The First Mindfulness Training

*Aware of the suffering caused by the destruction of life,
I am committed to cultivating compassion and learning ways
to protect the lives of people, animals, plants, and minerals. I am
determined not to kill, not to let others kill, and not to support any
act of killing in the world, in my thinking, and in my way of life.*

More and more people are beginning to realize that the survival of our planet depends on our sense of belonging— to all other humans, to dolphins caught in dragnets, to chickens and pigs and calves raised in animal concentration camps, to redwoods and rainforests, to kelp beds in our oceans, and to the ozone layer. More and more people are becoming aware that every act that affirms this belonging is a moral act of worship, the fulfillment of a precept written in every human heart.

—Brother David Steindl-Rast

Life is precious. It is everywhere, inside us and all around us; it has so many forms. The First Mindfulness Training is born from the awareness that lives everywhere are being destroyed. We see the suffering caused by the destruction of life, and we vow to cultivate compassion and use it as a source of energy for the protection of people, animals, plants, and minerals. The First Mindfulness Training is a training of compassion, *karuna*—the ability to remove suffering and transform it. When we see suffering, compassion is born in us.

It is important for us to stay in touch with the suffering of the world. We need to nourish that awareness through many means—sounds, images, direct contact, visits, and so on—in order to keep compassion alive in us. But we must be careful not to take in too much. Any remedy must be taken in the proper dosage. We need to stay in touch with suffering only to the extent that we will not forget, so that compassion will flow within us and be a source of energy for our actions. If we use anger at injustice as the source for our energy, we may do something harmful, something that we will later regret. According to Buddhism, compassion is the only source of energy that is useful and safe. With compassion, your energy is born from insight; it is not blind energy.

We humans are made entirely of non-human elements, such as plants, minerals, earth, clouds, and sunshine. For our practice to be deep and true, we must include the ecosystem. If the environment is destroyed, humans will be destroyed, too. Protecting human life is not possible without also protecting the lives of animals, plants, and minerals. The Diamond Sutra teaches us that it is impossible to distinguish between sentient and non-sentient beings. This is one of many ancient Buddhist texts that teach deep ecology. Every Buddhist practitioner should be a protector of the environment. Minerals have their own lives, too. In Buddhist monasteries, we chant, "Both sentient and non-sentient beings will realize full enlightenment." The First Mindfulness Training is the practice of protecting all lives, including the lives of minerals.

"I am determined not to kill, not to let others kill, and not to support any act of killing in the world, in my thinking, and in my way of life." We cannot support any act of killing; no killing can be justified. But not to kill is not enough. We must also learn ways to prevent others from killing. We cannot say, "I am not responsible. They did it. My hands are clean." If you were in Germany during the time of the Nazis, you could not say, "They did it. I did not." If, during the Gulf War, you did not say or do anything to try to stop the killing, you were not practicing this training. Even if what you said or did failed to stop the war, what is important is that you tried, using your insight and compassion.

It is not just by not killing with your body that you observe the First Mindfulness Training. If in your thinking you allow the killing to go on, you also break this training. We must be determined not to condone killing, even in our minds. According to the Buddha, the mind is the base of all actions. It is most dangerous to kill in the mind. When you believe, for example, that yours is the only way for humankind and that everyone who follows another way is your enemy, millions of people could be killed because of that idea.

Thinking is at the base of everything. It is important for us to put an eye of awareness into each of our thoughts. Without a correct understanding of a situation or a person, our thoughts can be misleading and create confusion, despair, anger, or hatred. Our most important task is to develop correct insight. If we see deeply into the nature of interbeing, that all things inter-are, we will stop blaming, arguing, and killing, and we will become friends with everyone. To practice nonviolence, we must first of all learn ways to deal peacefully with ourselves. If we create true harmony within ourselves, we will know how to deal with family, friends, and associates.

When we protest against a war, for example, we may assume that we are a peaceful person, a representative of peace, but this isn't necessarily true. If we look deeply, we will observe that the roots of war are in the unmindful ways we have been living. We have not sown enough seeds of peace and understanding in ourselves and others, therefore we are co-responsible. A more holistic approach is the way of interbeing. The essential nature of interbeing is understanding that "this is like this, because that is like that." We only exist in this interconnected way. This is the way of understanding and love. With this insight, we can see clearly and be more effective. Then we can go to a demonstration and say, "This war is unjust, destructive, and not worthy of our great nation." This is far more effective than simply angrily condemning others. Acting and speaking out of anger almost always accelerates the damage.

All of us have pain inside. We feel angry and frustrated, and we need to find someone willing to listen to us who is capable of understanding our suffering. In Buddhist iconography, there is a bodhisattva named Avalokiteshvara who has one thousand arms and one thousand hands, and has an eye in the palm of each hand. One thousand hands represent action, and the eye in each hand represents understanding. When you understand a situation or a person, any action you do will help and will not cause more suffering. When you have an eye in your hand, you will know how to practice true nonviolence.

To practice nonviolence, first of all we have to practice it within ourselves. In each of us, there is a certain amount of violence and a certain amount of nonviolence. Depending on our state of being, our response to things will be more or less nonviolent. Even if we take pride in being vegetarian, for example, we have to acknowledge that the water in which we boil our vegetables contains many tiny microorganisms. We cannot be completely nonviolent, but by being vegetarian, we are going in the direction of nonviolence. If we want to head north, we can use the North Star to guide us, but it is impossible to arrive at the North Star. Our effort is only to proceed in that direction.

Anyone can practice some nonviolence, even army generals. To help soldiers move in a nonviolent direction, we have to be in touch with them. If we divide reality into two camps—the violent and the nonviolent—and stand in one camp while attacking the other, the world will never have peace. We will always blame and condemn those we feel are responsible for wars and social injustice, without recognizing the degree of violence in ourselves. We must work on ourselves and also work with those we condemn if we want to have a real impact.

It never helps to draw a line and dismiss some people as enemies, even those who act violently. We have to approach them with love in our hearts and do our best to help them move in a direction of nonviolence. If we work for peace out of anger, we will never succeed. Peace is not an end. It can never come about through non-peaceful means.

Most important is to *become* nonviolence, so that when a situation presents itself, we will not create more suffering. To practice nonviolence, we need gentleness, loving kindness, compassion, joy, and equanimity directed to our bodies, our feelings, and other people. With mindfulness—the practice of peace—we can begin by working to transform the wars in ourselves. There are techniques for doing this. Conscious breathing is one. Every time we feel upset, we can stop what we are doing, refrain from saying anything, and breathe in and out several times, aware of each in-breath and each out-breath. If we are still upset, we can go for walking meditation, mindful of each slow step and each breath we take.

By cultivating peace within, we bring about peace in society. It depends on us. To practice peace in ourselves is to minimize the numbers of wars between this and that feeling, or this and that perception, and we can then have real peace with others as well, including the members of our own family.

I am often asked, "What if you are practicing nonviolence and someone breaks into your house and tries to kidnap your daughter or kill your husband? What should you do? Should you still act in a nonviolent way?" The answer depends on your state of being. If you are prepared, you may react calmly and intelligently, in the most nonviolent way possible. But to be ready to react with intelligence and nonviolence, you have to train yourself in advance. It may take ten years, or longer. If you wait until the time of crisis to ask the question, it will be too late. A this-or-that kind of answer would be superficial. At that crucial moment, even if you know that nonviolence is better than violence, if your understanding is only intellectual and not in your whole being, you will not act nonviolently. The fear and anger in you will prevent you from acting in the most nonviolent way.

We have to look deeply every day to practice this training well. Every time we buy or consume something, we may be condoning some form of killing. While practicing the protection of humans, animals, plants, and minerals, we know that we are protecting ourselves. We feel in permanent and loving touch with all species on Earth. We are protected by the mindfulness and loving kindness of the Buddha and many generations of communities, of *Sangha*s, who also practice this mindfulness training. This energy of loving kindness brings us the feeling of safety, health, and joy, and this becomes real the moment we make the decision to receive and practice the First Mindfulness Training.

Feeling compassion is not enough. We have to learn to express it. That is why love must go together with understanding. Understanding and insight show us how to act. Our real enemy is forgetfulness. If we nourish mindfulness every day and water the seeds of peace in ourselves and those around us, we become alive, and we can help ourselves and others realize peace and compassion.

Life is so precious, yet in our daily lives we are usually carried away by our forgetfulness, anger, and worries, lost in the past, unable to touch life in the present moment. When we are truly alive, everything we do or touch is a miracle. To practice mindfulness is to return to life in the present moment. The practice of the First Mindfulness Training is a celebration of reverence for life. When we appreciate and honor the beauty of life, we will do everything in our power to protect all life.

# The Second Mindfulness Training

*Aware of the suffering caused by exploitation, social injustice,*
*stealing, and oppression, I am committed to cultivating loving*
*kindness and learning ways to work for the well-being of people,*
*animals, plants, and minerals. I will practice generosity by*
*sharing my time, energy, and material resources with those who*
*are in real need. I am determined not to steal and not to possess*
*anything that should belong to others. I will respect the property*
*of others, but I will prevent others from profiting from human*
*suffering or the suffering of other species on Earth.*

There is a wonderful aspect to the mindfulness trainings:
they are actually impossible to keep! To refrain from harming others? What a profound practice! We receive the Five
Mindfulness Trainings knowing that by doing so we are
opening up to our own failure. We cannot fix the world, we
cannot even fix our own life. By accepting failure we
express our willingness to begin again, time after time. By
recognizing failure we change, renew, adapt, listen, and

grow. It is only by practicing without expectation of success that we can ever truly open to the world, to suffering and to joy. What extraordinary courage there is in risking losing what you know for the sake of the unknown; risking what you think you are capable of for the sake of your true capability! What profound freedom—not having to get it right all the time, not having to live for the sake of appearance! By opening to our own failure, we open to the magnificence of the unknown, participating unconditionally, renewing our life.

—Caitriona Reed

EXPLOITATION, social injustice, and stealing come in many forms. Oppression is one form of stealing that causes much suffering both here and in the Third World. The moment we vow to cultivate loving kindness, loving kindness is born in us, and we make every effort to stop exploitation, social injustice, stealing, and oppression.

In the First Mindfulness Training, we found the word "compassion." In the second, we find the words "loving kindness." Compassion and loving kindness are the two aspects of love taught by the Buddha. Compassion, *karuna* in Sanskrit, is the intention and capacity to relieve the suffering of another person or living being. Loving kindness, *maitri* in Sanskrit and *metta* in Pali, is the intention and capacity to bring joy and happiness to another person or living being. It was predicted by

Shakyamuni Buddha that the next Buddha will bear the name Maitreya, the Buddha of Love.

Even with maitri as a source of energy in ourselves, we still need to learn to look deeply in order to find ways to express it. We do it as individuals, and we learn ways to do it as a nation. To promote the well-being of people, animals, plants, and minerals, we have to come together as a community and examine our situation, exercising our intelligence and our ability to look deeply so that we can discover appropriate ways to express our maitri in the midst of real problems.

Suppose you want to help those who are suffering under a dictatorship. In the past you may have tried sending in troops to overthrow their government, but you have learned that when doing that, you cause the deaths of many innocent people, and even then, you might not overthrow the dictator. If you practice looking more deeply, with loving kindness, to find a better way to help these people without causing suffering, you may realize that the best time to help is before the country falls into the hands of a dictator. If you offer the young people of that country the opportunity to learn your democratic ways of governing by giving them scholarships to come to your country, that would be a good investment for peace in the future. If you had done that thirty years ago, the other country might be democratic now, and you would not have to bomb them or send in troops to "liberate" them. This is just one example of how looking deeply and learning can help us find ways to do things that are more in line with loving kindness. If we wait until the situation gets bad, it may be too late. If we practice the mindfulness trainings together with politicians, soldiers, businesspeople, lawyers, legislators, artists, writers, and

teachers, we can find the best ways to practice compassion, loving kindness, and understanding.

It requires time to practice generosity. We may want to help
those who are hungry, but we are caught in the problems of our
own daily lives. Sometimes, one pill or a little rice could save
the life of a child, but we do not take the time to help, because
we think we do not have the time. In Ho Chi Minh City, for example, there are street children who call themselves "the dust
of life." They are homeless, and they wander the streets by day
and sleep under trees at night. They scavenge in garbage heaps
to find things like plastic bags they can sell for one or two cents
per pound. The nuns and monks in Ho Chi Minh City have
opened their temples to these children, and if the children
agree to stay four hours in the morning—learning to read and
write and playing with the monks and nuns—they are offered
a vegetarian lunch. Then they can go to the Buddha hall for a
nap. (In Vietnam, we always take naps after lunch; it is so hot.
When the Americans came, they brought their practice of
working eight hours, from nine to five. Many of us tried, but we
could not do it. We desperately need our naps after lunch.)

Then, at two o'clock, there is more teaching and playing with
the children, and children who stay for the afternoon receive
dinner. The temple does not have a place for them to sleep
overnight. In our community in France, we have been supporting these nuns and monks. It costs only twenty cents for a child
to have both lunch and dinner, and it will keep him from being
out on the streets, where he might steal cigarettes, smoke, use
delinquent language, and learn the worst behavior. By encour-
aging the children to go to the temple, we help prevent them
from becoming delinquent and entering prison later on. It

takes time to help these children, not much money. There are so many simple things like this we can do to help people, but because we cannot free ourselves from our situation and our lifestyle, we do nothing at all. We need to come together as a community, and, looking deeply, find ways to free ourselves so we can practice the Second Mindfulness Training.

The feeling of generosity and the capacity for being generous are not enough. We also need to express our generosity. We may feel that we don't have the time to make people happy—we say, "Time is money," but time is more than money. Life is for more than using time to make money. Time is for being alive, for sharing joy and happiness with others. The wealthy are often the least able to make others happy. Only those with time can do so.

I know a man named Bac Siêu in Thua Thiên province in Vietnam, who has been practicing generosity for fifty years; he is a living bodhisattva. With only a bicycle, he visits villages of thirteen provinces, bringing something for this family and something for that family. When I met him in 1965, I was a little too proud of our School of Youth for Social Service. We had begun to train three hundred workers, including monks and nuns, to go out to rural villages to help people rebuild homes and modernize local economies, health-care systems, and education. Eventually we had ten thousand workers throughout the country. As I was telling Bac Siêu about our projects, I was looking at his bicycle and thinking that with a bicycle he could help only a few people. But when the communists took over and closed our School, Bac Siêu continued, because his way of working was formless. Our orphanages, dispensaries, schools, and resettlement centers were all shut down or taken by the government.

Thousands of our workers had to stop their work and hide. But Bac Siêu had nothing to take. He was truly a bodhisattva, working for the well-being of others. I feel more humble now concerning the ways of practicing generosity.

The war in Vietnam created many thousands of orphans. Instead of raising money to build orphanages, we sought people in the West to sponsor a child. We found families in the villages to each take care of one orphan, then we sent $6 every month to that family to feed the child and send him to school. Whenever possible, we tried to place the child in the family of an aunt, an uncle, or a grandparent. With just $6, the child was fed and sent to school, and the rest of the children in the family were also helped. Children benefit from growing up in a family. Being in an orphanage can be like being in the army—children do not grow up naturally. If we look for and learn ways to practice generosity, we will improve all the time.

When you practice one mindfulness training deeply, you will discover that you are practicing all five. The First Mindfulness Training is about taking life, which is a form of stealing—stealing the most precious thing someone has, her life. When we meditate on the Second Mindfulness Training, we see that stealing, in the forms of exploitation, social injustice, and oppression, are acts of killing—killing slowly by exploitation, by maintaining social injustice, and by political and economic oppression. Therefore, the Second Mindfulness Training has much to do with the mindfulness training of not killing. We see the "interbeing" nature of the first two mindfulness trainings. This is true of all five mindfulness trainings. Some people formally receive just one or two mindfulness trainings. I don't mind, because if you practice one or two mindfulness trainings deeply, all five mindfulness trainings will be observed.

Instead of stealing, exploiting, or oppressing, we practice generosity. In Buddhism, we say there are three kinds of gifts. The first is the gift of material resources. The second is to help people rely on themselves, to offer them the technology and know-how to stand on their own feet. Helping people with the Dharma so they can transform their fear, anger, and depression belongs to the second kind of gift. The third is the gift of non-fear. We are afraid of many things. We feel insecure, afraid of being alone, afraid of sickness and dying. To help people not be destroyed by their fears, we practice the third kind of gift-giving.

The Bodhisattva Avalokiteshvara is someone who practices this extremely well. In the Heart Sutra, he teaches us the way to transform and transcend fear and ride on the waves of birth and death, smiling. He says that there is no production, no destruction, no being, no nonbeing, no increasing, and no decreasing. Hearing this helps us look deeply into the nature of reality to see that birth and death, being and nonbeing, coming and going, increasing and decreasing are all just ideas that we ascribe to reality, while reality transcends all concepts. When we realize the interbeing nature of all things—that even birth and death are just concepts—we transcend fear.

In 1991, I visited a friend in New York who was dying, Alfred Hassler. We had worked together in the peace movement for almost thirty years. Alfred looked as though he had been waiting for me to come before dying, and he died only a few hours after our visit. I went with my closest colleague, Sister Chân Không. Alfred was not awake when we arrived. His daughter Laura tried to wake him up, but she couldn't. So I asked Sister Chân Không to sing Alfred the "Song of No Coming and No Going": "These eyes are not me, I am not caught by these eyes. This body is not me, I am not caught by this body. I am life without boundaries. I have never been born, I will never die." The idea is taken from the Samyutta Nikaya. She sang so beautifully, and I saw streams of tears running down the faces of Alfred's wife and children. They were tears of understanding, and they were very healing.

Suddenly, Alfred came back to himself. Sister Chân Không began to practice what she had learned from studying the sutra titled Teachings to Be Given to the Sick. She said, "Alfred, do you remember the times we worked together?" She evoked many happy memories we had shared together, and Alfred was able to remember each of them. Although he was obviously in pain, he smiled. This practice brought results right away. When a person is suffering from so much physical pain, we sometimes can alleviate his suffering by watering the seeds of happiness that are in him. A kind of balance is restored, and he will feel less pain.

All the while, I was practicing massage on his feet, and I asked him whether he felt my hands on his body. When you are dying, areas of your body become numb, and you feel as if you have lost those parts of your body. Doing massage in mindfulness, gently, gives the dying person the feeling that he is alive and being cared for. He knows that love is there. Alfred nodded, and his eyes seemed to say, "Yes, I feel your hands. I know my foot is there."

Sister Chân Không asked, "Do you know we learned a lot

from you when we lived and worked together? The work you began, many of us are continuing to do. Please don't worry about anything." She told him many things like that, and he seemed to suffer less. At one point, he opened his mouth and said, "Wonderful, wonderful." Then, he sank back to sleep.

Before we left, we encouraged the family to continue these practices. The next day I learned that Alfred passed away just five hours after our visit. This was a kind of gift that belongs to the third category. If you can help people feel safe, less afraid of life, people, and death, you are practicing the third kind of gift.

During my meditation, I had a wonderful image—the shape of a wave, its beginning and its end. When conditions are sufficient, we perceive the wave, and when conditions are no longer sufficient, we do not perceive the wave. Waves are only made of water. We cannot label the wave as existing or nonexisting. After what we call the death of the wave, nothing is gone, nothing is lost. The wave has been absorbed into other waves, and somehow, time will bring the wave back again. There is no increasing, decreasing, birth, or death. When we are dying, if we think that everyone else is alive and we are the only person dying, our feeling of loneliness may be unbearable. But if we are able to visualize hundreds of thousands of people dying with us, our dying may become serene and even joyful. "I am dying in community. Millions of living beings are also dying in this very moment. I see myself together with millions of other living beings; we die in the Sangha. At the same time, millions of beings are coming to life. All of us are doing this together. I have been born, I am dying. We participate in the whole event as a Sangha." That is what I saw in my meditation. In the Heart

Sutra, Avalokiteshvara shares this kind of insight and helps us transcend fear, sorrow, and pain. The gift of non-fear brings about a transformation in us.

The Second Mindfulness Training is a deep practice. We speak of time, energy, and material resources, but time is not only for energy and material resources. Time is for being with others—being with a dying person or with someone who is suffering. Being really present for even five minutes can be a very important gift. Time is not just to make money. It is to produce the gift of Dharma and the gift of non-fear.

# The Third Mindfulness Training

*Aware of the suffering caused by sexual misconduct, I am committed to cultivating responsibility and learning ways to protect the safety and integrity of individuals, couples, families, and society. I am determined not to engage in sexual relations without love and a long-term commitment. To preserve the happiness of myself and others, I am determined to respect my commitments and the commitments of others. I will do everything in my power to protect children from sexual abuse and to prevent couples and families from being broken by sexual misconduct.*

We have to look at the structures of male dominance and the exploitation of women worldwide. The structures of patriarchal greed, hatred, and delusion are interrelated with the violence in the world. Modern militarism is also closely associated with patriarchy. Buddhist practice points toward the development of full and balanced human beings, free from the socially-learned "masculine" and "feminine" patterns of thought, speech, and behavior, in touch with both aspects of themselves.

—Sulak Sivaraksa

S O MANY individuals, children, couples, and families have been destroyed by sexual misconduct. To practice the Third Mindfulness Training is to heal ourselves and heal our society. This is mindful living.

The Fifth Mindfulness Training—not to consume alcohol, toxins, or drugs—and the Third Mindfulness Training are linked. Both concern destructive and destabilizing behavior. These trainings are the right medicine to heal us. We need only to observe ourselves and those around us to see the truth. Our stability and the stability of our families and society cannot be obtained without the practice of these two trainings. If you look at individuals and families who are unstable and unhappy, you will see that many of them do not practice these trainings. You can make the diagnosis by yourself and then know that the medicine is there. Practicing these trainings is the best way to restore stability in the family and in society. For many people, this mindfulness training is easy to practice, but for others, it is quite difficult. It is important for these people to come together and share their experiences.

In the Buddhist tradition, we speak of the oneness of body and mind. Whatever happens to the body also happens to the mind. The sanity of the body is the sanity of the mind; the violation of the body is the violation of the mind. When we are angry, we may think that we are angry in our feelings, not in our body, but that is not true. When we love someone, we want to be close to him physically, but when we are angry at someone, we don't want to touch or be touched by that person. We cannot say that body and mind are separate.

A sexual relationship is an act of communion between body

and spirit. This is a very important encounter, not to be done in a casual manner. You know that in your soul there are certain areas—memories, pain, secrets—that are private, that you would only share with the person you love and trust the most. You do not open your heart and show it to just anyone. In the imperial city, there is a zone you cannot approach called the forbidden city; only the king and his family are permitted to circulate there. There is a place like that in your soul that you do not allow anyone to approach except the one you trust and love the most.

The same is true of our body. Our bodies have areas that we do not want anyone to touch or approach unless she is the one we respect, trust, and love the most. When we are approached casually or carelessly, with an attitude that is less than tender, we feel insulted in our body and soul. Someone who approaches us with respect, tenderness, and utmost care is offering us deep communication, deep communion. It is only in that case that we will not feel hurt, misused, or abused, even a little. This cannot be attained unless there is true love and commitment. Casual sex cannot be described as love. Love is deep, beautiful, and whole.

True love contains respect. In my tradition, husband and wife are expected to respect each other like guests, and when you practice this kind of respect, your love and happiness will continue for a long time. In sexual relationships, respect is one of the most important elements. Sexual communion should be like a rite, a ritual performed in mindfulness with great respect, care, and love. If you are motivated by some desire, that is not love. Desire is not love. Love is something much more responsible. It has care in it.

We have to restore the meaning of the word "love." We have been using it in a careless way. When we say, "I love hamburgers," we are not talking about love. We are talking about our appetite, our desire for hamburgers. We should not dramatize our speech and misuse words like that. We make words like "love" sick that way. We have to make an effort to heal our language by using words carefully. The word "love" is a beautiful word. We have to restore its meaning.

If love is real, we do not need long- or short-term commitments, or even a wedding ceremony. True love includes the sense of responsibility, accepting the other person as he is, with all his strengths and weaknesses. If we like only the best things in the person, that is not love. We have to accept his weaknesses and bring our patience, understanding, and energy to help him transform. Love is maitri, the capacity to bring joy and happiness, and karuna, the capacity to transform pain and suffering. This kind of love can only be good for people. It cannot be described as negative or destructive. It is safe. It guarantees everything.

The expression "long-term commitment" helps people understand the word "love." In the context of real love, commitment can only be long-term. It doesn't make any sense to say: "I want to love you. I want to help you. I want to care for you. I want you to be happy. I want to work for happiness. But just for a few days." That cannot be described as love. Many of us are afraid of commitment, whether to the mindfulness trainings, to our partners, or to anything else. We want freedom. But love, for ourselves and others, is a lifetime commitment.

Some relationships, such as our relationships with our children and our parents, are long-term commitments from birth.

You have to make a long-term commitment to love your son deeply and help him through the journey of life as long as you are alive. You cannot just say, "I don't love you anymore." When you have a good friend, you also make a long-term commitment. You need her. How much more so with someone who wants to share your life, your soul, your body. The phrase long-term commitment cannot express the depth of love, but it helps people understand.

But a long-term commitment between two people is only a beginning. When we are committing to being in a romantic relationship with someone, we also need the support of friends and other people. Regardless of whether you can have or choose to have a wedding ceremony, what is important is that your commitment to your partner is witnessed by many friends and both of your families. With the support of your community, your Sangha, your commitment to each other is stronger and more able to withstand difficulties.

In romantic love, your strong feelings for each other are very important, but they are not enough to sustain your happiness. Without other elements, what you describe as love may turn into something sour rather soon. The support of friends and family coming together weaves a kind of web. The strength of your feelings is only one of the strands of that web. Supported by many elements, the couple will be solid, like a tree. If a tree wants to be strong, it needs a number of roots sent deep into the soil. If a tree has only one root, it may be blown over by the wind. The life of a couple also needs to be supported by many elements—families, friends, ideals, practice, and Sangha.

In Plum Village, the practice community where I live in France, every time we have a wedding ceremony, we invite the whole community to celebrate and bring support to the couple. After the ceremony, on every full moon day, the couple recites the Five Awarenesses together, remembering that friends everywhere are supporting their relationship to be stable, long-lasting, and happy.* Whether or not your relationship is bound by law, it will be stronger and more long-lasting if made in the presence of a Sangha—friends who love you and want to support you in the spirit of understanding and loving kindness.

Love can be a kind of sickness. In the West and in Asia, we have the word "lovesick." What makes us sick is attachment. Although it is a sweet internal formation, this kind of love with attachment is like a drug. It makes us feel wonderful, but once we are addicted, we cannot have peace. We cannot study, do our daily work, or sleep. We only think of the object of our love. We are sick with love. This kind of love is linked to our willingness to possess and monopolize. We want the object of our love to be entirely ours and only for us. It is totalitarian. We do not want anyone to prevent us from being with him. This kind of love can be described as a prison, where we lock up our beloved and create only suffering for her. The one who is loved is deprived of freedom—of the right to be herself and enjoy life. This kind of love cannot be described as maitri or karuna. It is

---

* The Five Awarenesses are: 1. We are aware that all generations of our ancestors and all future generations are present in us. 2. We are aware of the expectations that our ancestors, our children, and their children have of us. 3. We are aware that our joy, peace, freedom, and harmony are the joy, peace, freedom, and harmony of our ancestors, our children, and their children. 4. We are aware that understanding is the very foundation of love. 5. We are aware that blaming and arguing never help us and only create a wider gap between us; that only understanding, trust, and love can help us change and grow.

only the willingness to make use of the other person in order to satisfy our own needs.

When you have sexual energy that makes you feel unhappy, as though you are losing your inner peace, you should know how to practice so that you do not do things that will bring suffering to other people or yourself. We have to learn about this. In Asia, we say there are three sources of energy—sexual, breath, and spirit. Sexual energy, called *tinh* in Vietnamese, is the first. When you have more sexual energy than you need, there will be an imbalance in your body and in your being. You need to know how to reestablish the balance, or you may act irresponsibly. According to Taoism and Buddhism, there are practices to help reestablish that balance, such as meditation or martial arts. You can learn the ways to channel your sexual energy into deep realizations in the domains of art and meditation.

The second source of energy is *khi*, breath energy. Life can be described as a process of burning. In order to burn, every cell in our body needs nutrition and oxygen. In his Fire Sermon, the Buddha said, "The eyes are burning, the nose is burning, the body is burning." In our daily lives, we have to cultivate our energy by practicing proper breathing. We benefit from the air and its oxygen, so we have to be sure that non-polluted air is available to us. Some people cultivate their khi by refraining from smoking and talking, or by practicing conscious breathing after talking a lot. When you speak, take the time to breathe. At Plum Village, every time we hear the bell of mindfulness, everyone stops what they are doing and breathes consciously three times. We practice this way to cultivate and preserve our khi energy.

The third source of energy is *thân*, spirit energy. When you don't sleep at night, you lose some of this kind of energy. Your nervous system becomes exhausted and you cannot study or practice meditation well, or make good decisions. You don't have a clear mind because of lack of sleep or from worrying too much. Worry and anxiety drain this source of energy.

So don't worry. Don't stay up too late. Keep your nervous system healthy. Prevent anxiety. These kinds of practices cultivate the third source of energy. You need this source of energy to practice meditation well. A spiritual breakthrough requires the power of your spirit energy, which comes about through concentration and knowing how to preserve this source of energy. When you have strong spirit energy, you only have to focus it on an object, and you will have a breakthrough. If you don't have thân, the light of your concentration will not shine brightly, because the light emitted is very weak.

According to Asian medicine, the power of thân is linked to the power of tinh. When we expend our sexual energy, it takes time to restore it. In Chinese medicine, when you want to have a strong spirit and concentration, you are advised to refrain from having sexual relationships or overeating. You will be given herbs, roots, and medicine to enrich your source of thân, and, during the time you are taking this medicine, you are asked to refrain from sexual relationships. If your source of spirit is weak and you continue to have sexual relations, it is said that you cannot recover your spirit energy. Those who practice meditation should try to preserve their sexual energy, because they need it during meditation. If you are an artist, you may wish to practice channeling your sexual energy together with your spirit energy into your art.

During his struggle against the British, Gandhi undertook

many hunger strikes, and he recommended to his friends who joined him on these fasts not to have sexual intercourse. When you fast for many days, if you have sexual relations, you may die; you have to preserve your energies. Thich Tri Quang, my friend who fasted for 100 days in the hospital in Saigon in 1966, knew very well that not having sexual intercourse was very basic. Of course, as a monk, he did not have any problem with that. He also knew that speaking is an energy drain, so he refrained from speaking. If he needed something, he said it in one or two words or wrote it down. Writing, speaking, or making too many movements draws from these three sources of energy. So, the best thing is to lie down on your back and practice deep breathing. This brings into you the vitality that you need to survive a hundred-day hunger strike. If you don't eat, you cannot replenish this energy. If you refrain from studying, doing research, or worrying, you can preserve these resources. These three sources of energy are linked to each other. By practicing one, you help the other. That is why *anapanasati*, the practice of conscious breathing, is so important for our spiritual life. It helps with all of our sources of energy.

Monks and nuns do not engage in sexual relationships because they want to devote their energy to having a breakthrough in meditation. They learn to channel their sexual energy to strengthen their spirit energy for the breakthrough. They also practice deep breathing to increase the spirit energy. Since they live alone, without a family, they can devote most of their time to meditation and teaching, helping the people who provide them with food, shelter, and so on. They have contact with the population in the village in order to share the Dharma. Since they do not have a house or a family to care for, they have the time and space to do the things they like the most—walking, sitting, breathing, and helping fellow monks, nuns, and laypeople. Monks and nuns don't marry in order to preserve their time and energy for the practice.

"Responsibility" is the key word in the Third Mindfulness Training. In a community of practice, if there is no sexual misconduct, if the community practices this mindfulness training well, there will be stability and peace. We all need to respect, support, and protect each other as Dharma brothers and sisters. If we don't practice this mindfulness training, we may become irresponsible and create trouble in the community and in the community at large. We have all seen this. If a teacher cannot refrain from sleeping with one of her students, she will destroy everything, possibly for several generations. We need mindfulness in order to have that sense of responsibility. We refrain from sexual misconduct because we are responsible for the well-being of so many people. If we are irresponsible, we can destroy everything. By practicing this mindfulness training, we keep the Sangha beautiful.

In sexual relationships, people can get wounded. Practicing this mindfulness training is to prevent ourselves and others from being wounded. Often we think it is the woman who receives the wound, but men also get deeply wounded. We have to be very careful, especially in short-term commitments. The practice of the Third Mindfulness Training is a very strong way of restoring stability and peace in ourselves, our family, and our society. We should take the time to discuss problems relating to the practice of this mindfulness training, like loneliness, advertising, and even the sex industry.

The feeling of loneliness is universal in our society. There is no communication between ourselves and other people, even in the family, and our feeling of loneliness pushes us into having sexual relationships. We believe in a naive way that having a sexual relationship will make us feel less lonely, but it isn't true. When there is not enough communication with another person on the level of the heart and spirit, a sexual relationship will only widen the gap and destroy us both. Our relationship will be stormy, and we will make each other suffer. The belief that having a sexual relationship will help us feel less lonely is a kind of superstition. We should not be fooled by it. In fact, we will feel more lonely afterwards.

The union of the two bodies can only be positive when there is understanding and communion on the level of the heart and the spirit. Even between romantic partners, if the communion on the level of heart and spirit does not exist, the coming together of the two bodies will only separate you further. When that is the case, I recommend that you refrain from having sexual relationships and first try to make a breakthrough in communication.

There are two Vietnamese words we translate into English as "love." They are *tinh* and *nghia*. In tinh, you find elements of passion. It can be very deep, absorbing the whole of your being. Nghia, another Vietnamese word for love, is a kind of continuation of tinh. With nghia, you feel much calmer, more understanding, more willing to sacrifice to make the other person happy, and more faithful. You are not as passionate as in tinh, but your love is deeper and more solid. Nghia will keep you and the other person together for a long time. It is the result of living together and sharing difficulties and joy over time.

You begin with passion, but, living with each other, you

encounter difficulties, and as you learn to deal with them, your love deepens. Although the passion diminishes, nghia increases all the time. Nghia is a deeper love, with more wisdom, more interbeing, more unity. You understand the other person better. You and that person become one reality. Nghia is like a fruit that is already ripe. It does not taste sour anymore; it is only sweet.

In nghia, you feel gratitude for the other person. "Thank you for having chosen me. Thank you for being my partner. There are so many people in society, why have you chosen me? I am very thankful." That is the beginning of nghia, the sense of thankfulness for your having chosen me as your companion to share the best things in yourself, as well as your suffering and your happiness.

When we live together, we support each other. We begin to understand each other's feelings and difficulties. When the other person has shown his understanding of our problems, difficulties, and deep aspirations, we feel thankful for that understanding. When you feel understood by someone, you stop being unhappy. Happiness is, first of all, feeling understood. "I am grateful because you have proved that you understand me. While I was having difficulty and remained awake deep into the night, you took care of me. You showed me that my well-being is your own well-being. You did the impossible in order to bring about my well-being. You took care of me in a way that no one else in this world could have. For that I am grateful to you."

If the couple lives with each other for a long time, until their hair becomes white and their teeth fall out, it is because of nghia, and not because of tinh. Tinh is passionate love. Nghia is the kind of love that has a lot of understanding and gratitude in it.

All love may begin by being passionate, especially for younger people. But in the process of living together, they have to learn and practice love, so that selfishness—the tendency to possess—will diminish, and the elements of understanding and gratitude will settle in, little by little, until their love becomes nourishing, protecting, and reassuring. With nghia, you are very sure that the other person will take care of you and will love you until your teeth fall out and your hair becomes white. Nothing will assure you that the person will be with you for a long time except nghia. Nghia is built by both of you in your daily life.

To meditate is to look into the nature of our love to see the kind of elements that are in it. We cannot call our love just tinh or nghia, possessive love or altruistic love, because there may be elements of both in it. It may be ninety percent possessive love, three percent altruistic love, two percent gratitude, and so on. Look deeply into the nature of your love and find out. The happiness of the other person and your own happiness depend on the nature of your love. Of course you have love in you, but what is important is the nature of that love. If you realize that there is a lot of maitri and karuna in your love, that will be very reassuring. Nghia will be strong in it.

Children, if they observe deeply, will see that what keeps their parents together is nghia. If their parents take good care of each other, look after each other with calmness, tenderness, and care, nghia is the foundation of that care. That is the kind of love we really need for our family and for our society.

In practicing the Third Mindfulness Training, we need to

look into the nature of our love in order to see and not be fooled by our feelings. Sometimes we feel that we have love for the other person, but maybe that love is only an attempt to satisfy our own egoistic needs. Maybe we have not looked deeply enough to see the needs of the other person, including the need to be safe, protected. If we have that kind of breakthrough, we will realize that the other person needs our protection, and therefore we cannot look upon her just as an object of our desire. The other person should not be looked upon as a kind of commercial item.

Sex is used in our society as a means for selling products. We also have the sex industry. If we don't look at the other person as a human being, with the capacity of becoming a Buddha, we risk transgressing this mindfulness training. Therefore the practice of looking deeply into the nature of our love has a lot to do with the practice of the Third Mindfulness Training.

Adults who were molested as children continue to suffer very much. Everything they think, do, and say bears the mark of that wound. They want to transform themselves and heal their wound, and the best way to do this is to observe the Third Mindfulness Training. Because of their own experience, they can say, "As a victim of sexual abuse, I vow to protect all children and adults from sexual abuse." Our suffering becomes a kind of positive energy that will help us become a bodhisattva. We vow to protect all children and other people. And we also vow to help those who abuse children sexually, because they are sick and need our help. The ones who made us suffer become the object of our love and protection. The ones who will molest children in the future become the objects of our love and protection.

We see that until the sick people are protected and helped, children are going to continue to be abused sexually. We vow to help these people so that they will not molest children any longer. At the same time, we vow to help children. We take not only the side of children who are being molested, but the other side also. These molesters are sick, the products of an unstable society. They may be an uncle, an aunt, a grandparent, or a parent. They need to be observed, helped, and, if possible, healed. When we are determined to observe this mindfulness training, the energy that is born helps us transform into a bodhisattva, and that transformation may heal us even before we begin to practice. The best way for anyone who was molested as a child to heal is to take this mindfulness training and vow to protect children and adults who may be sick, who may be repeating the kind of destructive actions that will cause a child to be wounded for the rest of his life.

# The Fourth Mindfulness Training

DEEP LISTENING AND LOVING SPEECH

*Aware of the suffering caused by unmindful speech and the inability to listen to others, I am committed to cultivating loving speech and deep listening in order to bring joy and happiness to others and relieve others of their suffering. Knowing that words can create happiness or suffering, I am determined to speak truthfully, with words that inspire self-confidence, joy, and hope. I will not spread news that I do not know to be certain and will not criticize or condemn things of which I am not sure. I will refrain from uttering words that can cause division or discord, or that can cause the family or the community to break. I am determined to make all efforts to reconcile and resolve all conflicts, however small.*

Mindfulness is to accept whatever arises and to recognize it as such. At the root of my practice of ethics is the ability to accept that I am as much a potential murderer, thief, rapist, liar, and drug-abuser as those convicted of such offenses in prison. To practice ethics is to be able to accept the reality of such impulses—and let them go. To let them go means to allow them to follow their own nature of pass-ing away. For only when I affirm an impulse ("Yes, I hate that person!"), do I set in motion the train of events that culminates in verbal or physical action.

—Stephen Batchelor

THERE IS a saying in Vietnamese, "It doesn't cost anything to have loving speech." We only need to choose our words carefully, and we can make other people happy. To use words mindfully, with loving kindness, is to practice generosity. Therefore this training is linked directly to the Second Mindfulness Training. We can make many peo-ple happy just by practicing loving speech. Again, we see the in-terbeing nature of the Five Mindfulness Trainings.

Many people think they will be able to practice generosity only after they have accumulated a small fortune. I know young people who dream of getting rich so they can bring happiness to others: "I want to become a doctor or the president of a big company so I can make a lot of money and help many people." They do not realize that it is often more difficult to practice generosity after you are wealthy. If you are motivated by loving kindness and compassion, there are many ways to bring happi-ness to others right now, starting with kind speech. The way you speak to others can offer them joy, happiness, self-confidence, hope, trust, and enlightenment. Mindful speaking is a deep practice.

Avalokitesvara Bodhisattva is a person who has learned the art of listening and speaking deeply in order to help people let go of their fear, misery, and despair. He is the model of this practice, and the door he opens is called the "universal door." If we practice listening and speaking according to Avalokitesvara, we too will be able to open the universal door and bring joy, peace, and happiness to many people and alleviate their suffering.

The universal door manifests itself
in the voice of the rolling tide.
Hearing and practicing it, we become a child,
born from the heart of a lotus,
fresh, pure, and happy,
capable of speaking and listening
in accord with the universal door.
With only one drop of the water
of compassion
from the branch of the willow,
spring returns to the great Earth.

I learned this beautiful poem when I studied the Lotus Sutra at age sixteen. When you hear "the voice of the rolling tide," which is Avalokiteshvara's practice, symbolizing the universal door, you are transformed into a child born in the heart of a lotus. With only one drop of the water of compassion from the willow branch of the bodhisattva, spring returns to our dry Earth. The dry Earth means the world of suffering and misery. The drop of compassionate water is the practice of loving kind-ness, symbolized by the water on the willow branch. Avalokitehsvara is described by the Chinese, Vietnamese, Koreans, and Japanese as the person holding the willow branch. He dips the branch into the water of compassion of his heart, and wherever he sprinkles that water, everything is reborn. When he sprinkles it on dry, dead branches, they turn green. Dead branches also symbolize suffering and despair, and green vegetation symbolizes the return of peace and happiness. With only one drop of that water, spring returns to our great Earth.

In the "Universal Door" chapter of the Lotus Sutra, Avalokitesvara's voice is described in five ways: the wondrous voice, the voice of the world regarded, the *brahma* voice, the voice of the rising tide, and the voice of world surpassing. We should always keep these five voices in mind.

First, there is the wondrous voice. This is the kind of speaking that will open the universal door and make everything possible again. This voice is pleasant to hear. It is refreshing and brings calm, comfort, and healing to our soul. Its essence is compassion.

Second, there is the voice of the world regarded. The meaning of the word Avalokitesvara is "the one who looks deeply into the world and hears the cries of the world." This voice relieves our suffering and suppressed feelings, because it is the voice of someone who understands us deeply—our anguish, despair, and fear. When we feel understood, we suffer much less.

Third, there is the brahma voice. Brahma means noble—not just the ordinary voice of people, but the noble speech that springs forth from the willingness to bring happiness and remove suffering. Love, compassion, joy, and equanimity are the Four *Brahmavihara*s, noble dwellings of Buddhas and

bodhisattvas. If we want to live with Buddhas and bodhisattvas, we can dwell in these mansions.

During the time of the Buddha, the aim of the practice of
many people was to be born and to live together with Brahma.
It was similar to the Christian practice of wanting to go to
Heaven to be with God. "In my Father's house there are many
mansions," and you want to live in one of these mansions.* For
those who wanted to be with Brahma, the Buddha said, "Practice the four noble dwellings: love, compassion, joy, and equanimity." If we want to share one teaching of the Buddha with
our Christian friends, it would be the same: "God is love, compassion, joy, and impartiality." If you want to be with God,
practice these four dwellings. If you don't practice these four,
no matter how much you pray or talk about being with God,
going to Heaven will not be possible.

Fourth, the voice of the rising tide is the voice of the Buddhadharma. It is a powerful voice, the kind of voice that silences
all wrong views and speculations. It is the lion's roar that brings
absolute silence to the mountain and brings about transformation and healing.

Fifth, the voice of the world surpassing is the voice with
which nothing can be compared. This voice does not aim at
fame, profit, or a competitive edge. It is the thundering silence
that shatters all notions and concepts.

The wondrous voice, the voice of the world regarded, the
brahma voice, the voice of the rising tide, and the voice of the
world surpassing are the voices we are to be mindful of. If we
contemplate these five kinds of voices, we assist Avalokitesh-

---

* New Testament, John 14:2

vara in opening the universal door, the door of real listening and real speaking.

Because he lives a mindful life, always contemplating the world, and because he is the world regarder, Avalokitesvara notices a lot of suffering. He knows that much suffering is born from unmindful speech and the inability to listen to others; therefore he practices mindful, loving speech and listening deeply. Avalokitesvara can be described as the one who teaches us the best way to practice the Fourth Mindfulness Training.

Never in the history of humankind have we had so many means of communication—email, cell phones, faxes, television, radios, newspapers—but we still remain distant islands. There is so little communication between the members of one family, between the individuals in society, and between nations. We suffer from so many wars and conflicts. We surely have not cultivated the arts of listening and speaking. We don't know how to listen to each other. We have little ability to hold an intelligent or meaningful conversation. The universal door of communication has to be opened again. When we can't communicate, we get sick, and as our sickness increases, we suffer and spill our suffering on other people. We purchase the services of psychotherapists to listen to our suffering. Psychotherapists are human beings who are subject ot suffering like the rest of us. They may have problems with their partner, children, friends, society. They also have internal formations. They may have a lot of suffering that cannot be communicated to even the most beloved person in their life. How can they listen to our suffering and understand our suffering? Psychotherapists must be able to practice the universal door, deep listening and mindful speech, or they won't be able to help us or themselves.

Unless we look deeply into ourselves, this practice will not be easy. If there is a lot of suffering in you, it is difficult to listen to other people or to say nice things to them. First you have to look deeply into the nature of your anger, despair, and suffering to free yourself, so you can be available to others. Suppose your partner said something unkind on Monday and it hurt you. He used unmindful speech and does not have the ability to listen. If you reply right away out of your anger and suffering, you risk hurting him and making his suffering deeper. What should you do? If you suppress your anger or remain silent, that can hurt you, because if you try to suppress the anger in you, you are suppressing yourself. You will suffer later, and your suffering will bring more suffering to your partner.

The best immediate practice is to breathe in and out in order to calm your anger, to calm the pain: "Breathing in, I know that I am angry. Breathing out, I calm my feeling of anger." Just by breathing deeply on your anger, you will calm it. You are being mindful of your anger, not suppressing it. When you are calm enough, you may be able to use mindful speech. In a loving and mindful way, you can say, "Darling, I would like you to know that I am angry. What you just said hurt me a lot, and I want you to know that." Just saying that, mindfully and calmly, will give you some relief. Breathing mindfully to calm your anger, you will be able to tell the other person that you are suffering. During that moment, you are living your anger, touching it with the energy of mindfulness. You are not denying it at all.

Anger is an organic thing, like love. Anger can become love. Our compost can become a rose. If we know how to take care of our compost, we can transform it into a rose. Should we call the garbage negative or positive? It can be positive, if we know how to handle it. Anger is the same. It can be negative when we do not know how to handle it, but if we know how to handle our anger, it can be very positive. We do not need to throw anything away.

After you breathe in and out a number of times to recover your calmness, even if your anger is still there, you are mindful of it, and you can tell the other person that you are angry. You can also tell him that you would like to look deeply into it, and you would like him to look deeply into it also. Then you can make an appointment for an evening to look at it together. One person looking at the roots of your suffering is good, two people looking at it is better, and two people looking together is best.

I propose an evening a few nights later for two reasons. First, you are still angry, and if you began discussing it now, it may be too risky. You might say things that will make the situation worse. From now until that evening, you can practice looking deeply into the nature of your anger, and the other person can also. While driving the car, he might ask himself, "What is so serious? Why did she get so upset? There must be a reason." While driving, you will also have a chance to look deeply into it. Before that night, one or both of you may see the root of the problem and be able to tell the other and apologize. Then on that night, you can have a cup of tea together and enjoy each other. If you make an appointment, you will both have time to calm down and look deeply. This is the practice of meditation; it calms us and allows us to look deeply into the nature of our suffering.

When that night comes, if the suffering has not been transformed, you will be able to practice the art of Avalokiteshvara. You sit together and practice deep listening—one person expressing herself, while the other person listens deeply. When you speak, you tell the deepest kind of truth, and you practice loving speech. Only by using that kind of speech will there be a chance for the other person to understand and accept. While listening, you know that only with deep listening can you relieve the suffering of the other person. If you listen with just half an ear, you cannot do it. Your presence must be deep and real. Your listening must be of a good quality in order to relieve the other person of his suffering. This is the practice of the Fourth Mindfulness Training. You may want to make the appointment for Friday evening. When you neutralize that feeling Friday evening, you have Saturday and Sunday to enjoy being together.

Suppose you have some kind of internal formation regarding a member of your family or community, and you don't feel joyful being with that person. You can talk to her about simple things, but you don't feel comfortable talking with her about anything deep. Then one day, while doing housework, you notice that the other person is not doing anything at all, is not sharing the work that needs to be done, and you begin to feel uneasy. "Why am I doing so much and she isn't doing anything? She should be working." Because of this comparison, you lose your happiness. But instead of telling the other person, "Please, Sister, come and help with the work," you say to yourself, "She is an adult. Why should I have to say something to her? She should be more responsible!" You think that way because you already have some internal formation about the other person. The shortest way is always the direct way. "B" can go to "A" and say, "Sister, please come and help." But you do not do that. You keep it to yourself and blame the other person.

The next time the same thing happens, your feeling is even more intense. Your internal formation grows little by little, until you suffer so much that you need to talk about it with a third person. You are looking for sympathy in order to share the suffering. So, instead of talking directly to "A," you talk to "C." You look for "C" because you think that "C" is an ally who will agree that "A" is not behaving well at all.

If you are "C," what should you do? If you already have some internal formations concerning "A," you will probably be glad to hear that someone else feels the same. Talking to each other may make you feel better. You are becoming allies—"B" and "C" against "A." Suddenly "B" and "C" feel close to each other, and both of you feel some distance from "A." "A" will notice that.

"A" may be very nice. She would be capable of responding directly to "B" if "B" could express her feelings to her. But "A" does not know about "B's" resentment. She just feels some kind of cooling down between herself and "B," without knowing why. She notices that "B" and "C" are becoming close, while both of them look at her coldly. So she thinks, "If they don't want me, I don't need them." She steps farther back from them, and the situation worsens. A triangle has been set up.

If I were "C," first of all, I would listen to "B" attentively, understanding that "B" needs to share her suffering. Knowing that the direct way is the shortest way, I would encourage "B" to speak directly to "A." If "B" is unable to do this, I would offer to speak to "A" on "B's" behalf, either with "B" present, or alone.

But, most important, I would not transmit to anyone else what "B" tells me in confidence. If I am not mindful, I may tell others what I now know about "B's" feelings, and soon the family or the community will be a mess. If I do these things—encourage "B" to speak directly with "A" or speak with "A" on "B's" behalf, and not tell anyone else what "B" has told me—I will be able to break the triangle. This may help solve the problem, and bring peace and joy back into the family, the community, and the society.

Speech can be constructive or destructive. Mindful speaking can bring real happiness; unmindful speech can kill. When someone tells us something that makes us healthy and happy, that is the greatest gift she can give. Sometimes, someone says something to us that is so cruel and distressing that we want to go and commit suicide; we lose all hope, all our joie de vivre.

People kill because of speech. When you fanatically advocate an ideology, saying that this way of thinking or organizing society is the best, then if anyone stands in your way, you have to suppress or eliminate him. This is very much linked with the First Mindfulness Training—that kind of speech can kill not only one person, but many. When you believe in something that strongly, you can put millions of people into gas chambers. When you use speech to promote an ideology, urging people to kill in order to protect and promote your ideology, you can kill many millions. The First and Fourth of the Five Wonderful Mindfulness Trainings inter-are.

The Fourth Mindfulness Training is also linked to the Second Mindfulness Training, on stealing. Just as there is a "sex industry," there is also a "lying industry." Many people have to lie in order to succeed as politicians, or salespersons. A corporate director of communications told me that if he were allowed to tell the truth about his company's products, people would not buy them. He says positive things that he knows are not true about the products, and he refrains from speaking about the negative effects of them. He knows he is lying, and he feels terrible about it. So many people are caught in similar situations. In politics also, people lie to get votes. That is why we can speak of a "lying industry."

This training is also linked with the Third Mindfulness Training. When someone says, "I love you," it may be a lie. It may just be an expression of desire. And so much advertising is linked with sex.

In the Buddhist tradition, the Fourth Mindfulness Training is always described as refraining from these four actions:

1. Not telling the truth. If it's black, you say it's white.
2. Exaggerating. You make something up, or describe something as more beautiful than it actually is, or as ugly when it's not so ugly.
3. Forked tongue. You go to one person and say one thing and then you go to another person and say the opposite.
4. Filthy language. You insult or abuse people.

It is so important that we practice right speech with children, speech that inspires happiness, self-confidence, and hope in them. If you tell children they are good-for-nothing, they will suffer in the future. Always emphasize the positive, hopeful things with your children, and also with your spouse or partner.

Reconciliation is a deep practice that we can do with our listening and our mindful speech. To reconcile means to bring peace and happiness to nations, people, and members of our family. This is the work of a bodhisattva. In order to reconcile, you have to possess the art of deep listening, and you also have to master the art of loving speech. You have to refrain from aligning yourself with one party so that you are able to understand both parties. This is a difficult practice.

During the war in Vietnam, we tried to practice this. We tried not to align ourselves with either of the warring parties, the communists or the anticommunists. You will be able to help only if you stand above the conflict and see both the good and bad aspects of both sides. Doing this, you put yourself in a dangerous situation, because you may be hated by both sides. One side suspects that you are an instrument of the other side, and the other side suspects you are an instrument of the first side. You may be killed by both sides at the same time. That is exactly what many Buddhists in Vietnam suffered during the war. We did not align ourselves with the communists, but we did not align ourselves with the pro-American side either. We just wanted to be ourselves. We did not want any killing; we only wanted reconciliation. One side said that you cannot reconcile with the pro-Americans. The other side said that you cannot reconcile with the communists. If we had listened to both sides it would have been impossible to reconcile with anyone.

We trained social workers to go into the rural areas to help with health, economic, and educational problems, and we were suspected by both sides. Our work of reconciliation was not just the work of speaking, but also of acting. We tried to help the peasants find hope. We helped many refugees settle in new villages. We helped sponsor more than ten thousand orphans. We helped the peasants rebuild their destroyed villages. The work of reconciliation is not just diplomatic; it is concrete. At the same time, we were voicing the peace in our hearts. We said the people in one family must look upon each other as brothers and sisters and accept each other. They should not kill each other because of any ideology. That message was not at all popular in the situation of war.

My writings were censored by both sides. My poetry was seized by both sides. My friends printed one of my poetry books underground because the Saigon government would not allow its publication. Then the communist side attacked it on the radio saying that it was harmful to the struggle, probably motivated by the CIA. Nationalist policemen went into bookshops and confiscated the poems. In Huê, one kind policeman went into a Buddhist bookshop and said that this book should not be displayed; it should be hidden and given out only when someone asked for it. We were suppressed not only in our attempts to voice our concerns and propose ways to settle the problems between brothers and sisters, but also in our attempts to help people. Many of our social workers were killed and kidnapped by both sides. Each side suspected we were working for the other side. Some of our workers were assassinated by fanatic Catholics who suspected us of working for the communists, and some of our workers were taken away by the communist side. Our workers were quite popular in the countryside. They were very dedicated young men and women, including many young monks and nuns. They did not have salaries; they just wanted to serve and to practice Buddhism. In the situation of war, they brought their loving kindness, compassion, and good work, and received a small stipend to live. They went to the countryside without hoping for anything in return.

I remember a young man named An who specialized in helping peasants learn modern methods of raising chickens. He taught them disease prevention techniques. He was asked by a farmer, "How much do you earn from the government each month?" An said, "We don't earn anything from the government. In fact we are not from the government, we are from the temple. We are sent by the Buddhist temple to help you." An did not tell the farmer, who was not so sophisticated, that he was associated with the School of Youth for Social Service, founded by the Department of Social Work of the Unified Buddhist Church. That was too complicated, so he only said that he was sent by the temple.

"Why have you come here from the temple?"

An said, "We are performing merit." This is a very popular term in Buddhism.

The farmer was surprised. He said, "I have learned that in order to perform merit people go to the temple. Now why are you performing merit here?"

The young man said, "You know, my uncle, during these times the people suffer so much that even the Buddha has to come out here to help. We students of the Buddha are performing merit right here, where you suffer." That statement became the ground of our philosophy of social service, engaged Buddhism. The Buddha has to be in society. He cannot remain in the temple any longer, because people are suffering too much.

In a few years, we became very popular in the countryside of Vietnam. We did not have a lot of money, but because we worked in the way of performing merit, we were loved by the people. The communist side knew that and did not want us to be there, so they came to us during the night and asked who had given us permission to work there. Our workers said that we did not have permission from either the government or the communist side. We were just performing merit here. One time the communists gave the order for our social workers to evacuate an area, saying, "We will not be responsible for your safety if you stay beyond twenty-four hours."

Another time, some fanatics came from the government, unofficially, and asked our social workers if they were really social workers from the Buddhist community. Then they brought five of the students to the riverbank, and, after checking once more to be sure that they were Buddhist social workers, said, "We are sorry, but we have to kill you." They shot all five of them. We were suppressed by both sides during the night. They knew that if they suppressed us during the day, the peasants in the countryside would disapprove.

One grenade thrown into my room was deflected by a curtain. Another night, many grenades were thrown into our School's dormitories, killing two young workers, and injuring many others. One young man was paralyzed, and later treated in Germany. One young lady got more than 1,000 pieces of shrapnel in her body. She lost a lot of blood, and was saved by a Japanese friend who was helping us. Later, we were able to bring her to Japan for surgery. They tried to remove the small metal pieces, but 300 pieces that could not be taken out were left in her body.

One day when I was in Paris as representative of the Vietnamese Buddhist Peace Delegation, to be present at the Paris Peace Talks, I received a phone message from Saigon telling me that four social workers had just been shot and killed. I cried. It was I who had asked them to come and be trained as social workers. A friend who was there with me, said, "Thây, you are a kind of general leading a nonviolent army, and when your army is working for love and reconciliation, there surely will be casualties. There is no need to cry."

I said, "I am not a general. I am a human being. I need to cry." Six months later, I wrote a play about the deaths of these students, titled *The Path of Return Continues the Journey.**

The work of reconciliation is not diplomatic work alone. It is not because you travel and meet with dozens of foreign ministers that you do the work of reconciliation. You have to use your body, your time, and your life to do the work of reconciliation. You do it in many ways, and you can be suppressed by the people you are trying to help. You have to listen and understand the suffering of one side, and then go and listen to the suffering of the other side. Then you will be able to tell each side, in turn, about the suffering being endured by the other side. That kind of work is crucial, and it takes courage. We need many people who have the capacity of listening, in South Africa, in the Middle East, in Eastern Europe, and elsewhere.

The Fourth Mindfulness Training is a bodhisattva training. We need deep study to be able to practice it well, within ourselves, our families, our communities, our society, and the world. If, in the community, you see that someone is having difficulty with someone else, please help right away. The longer things drag on, the more difficult they are to solve. The best way to help is to practice mindful speech and deep listening. The Fourth Mindfulness Training can bring peace, understanding, and happiness to people. The universal door is a wonderful door. You will be reborn in a lotus flower and help others, including your family, your community, and your society, be born there also.

* See *Love in Action: Writings on Nonviolent Social Change* (Berkeley, CA: Parallax Press, 1993).

# The Fifth Mindfulness Training

*Aware of the suffering caused by unmindful consumption, I am committed to cultivating good health, both physical and mental, for myself, my family, and my society by practicing mindful eating, drinking, and consuming. I will ingest only items that preserve peace, well-being, and joy in my body, in my consciousness, and in the collective body and consciousness of my family and society. I am determined not to use alcohol or any other intoxicant or to ingest foods or other items that contain toxins, such as certain TV programs, magazines, books, films, and conversations. I am aware that to damage my body or my consciousness with these poisons is to betray my ancestors, my parents, my society, and future generations. I will work to transform violence, fear, anger, and confusion in myself and in society by practicing a diet for myself and for society. I understand that a proper diet is crucial for self-transformation and for the transformation of society.*

My own approach to food is to be curious and grateful. I would like to know where my food came from and who it was, plant or animal (Okra is a member of the Hibiscus family, originally from Africa! Tomatoes, Tobacco, Potatoes, Eggplant and Jimson weed are all Solanaceae together, with those trumpet-shaped flowers. I feel deepened by such facts.) . . . Our food is the field in which we daily explore our "harming" of the world, and how we deal with it. Clearly it will not do to simply stop here and declare that the world is pain and suffering and that we are all deluded. We are called instead to practice. In the course of our practice, we will not transform Reality, but we may transform ourselves. . . . The larger view is one that can acknowledge the simultaneous pain and beauty of this complexly interrelated real world.

—Gary Snyder

**M**INDFUL CONSUMPTION is the object of this mindfulness training. We are what we consume. If we look deeply into the items that we consume every day, we will come to know our own nature very well. We have to eat, drink, consume, but if we do it unmindfully, we may destroy our bodies and our consciousness, showing ingratitude toward our ancestors, our parents, and future generations.

Whenever we take a bath or a shower, we can look at our body and see that it is a gift from our parents and their parents. Even though many of us do not want to have much to do with our parents—they may have hurt us so much—when we look deeply, we see that we cannot drop all identification with them. As we wash each part of our body, we can ask ourselves, "To whom does this body belong? Who has transmitted this body to me? What has been transmitted?" Meditating this way, we will discover that there are three components: the transmitter, that which is transmitted, and the one who receives the transmission. The transmitter is our parents. We are the continuation of our parents and their ancestors. The object of transmission is our body itself. And the one who receives the transmission is us. If we continue to meditate on this, we will see clearly that the transmitter, the object transmitted, and the receiver are one. All three are present in our body. When we are deeply in touch with the present moment, we can see that all our ancestors and all future generations are present in us. Seeing this, we will know what to do and what not to do—for ourselves, our ancestors, our children, and their children.

If you think about your father, you might first feel very separate from him. You may be angry at him for many things. But the moment you understand and love your father, you realize the emptiness of transmission. You realize that to love yourself is to love your father, and to love your father is to love yourself. To keep your body and your consciousness healthy is to do it for your ancestors, your parents, and future generations. You do it for your society and for everyone, not just yourself. The first thing you have to bear in mind is that you are not practicing this as a separate entity. Whatever you ingest, you are doing it for everyone. All of your ancestors and all future generations are ingesting it with you. That is the true meaning of the emptiness of the transmission. The Fifth Mindfulness Training should be practiced in this spirit.

In modern life, people think that their body belongs to them and they can do anything they want to it. "We have the right to live our own lives." When you make such a declaration, the law supports you. This is one of the manifestations of individualism. But, according to the teaching of emptiness, your body is not yours. Your body belongs to your ancestors, your parents, and future generations. It also belongs to society and to all the other living beings. All of them have come together to bring about the presence of this body—the trees, clouds, everything. To keep your body healthy is to express gratitude to the whole cosmos, to all ancestors, and also not to betray the future generations. We practice this mindfulness training for the whole cosmos, the whole society. If we are healthy, everyone can benefit from it—not only everyone in the society of men and women, but everyone in the society of animals, plants, and minerals. This is a bodhisattva mindfulness training. When we practice the Five Mindfulness Trainings we are already on the path of a bodhisattva.

When we are able to get out of the shell of our small self and see that we are interrelated to everyone and everything, we see that our every act is linked with the whole of humankind, the whole cosmos. To keep yourself healthy is to be kind to your ancestors, your parents, the future generations, and also your society. Health is not only bodily health, but also mental health. The Fifth Mindfulness Training is about health and healing.

Even if all you are doing is to refrain from your usual habit of drinking a few glasses of wine a week, this is truly an act of a bodhisattva. You do it for everyone. At a reception, when someone offers you a glass of wine, you can smile and decline gently, with a smile. This is very helpful. You set an example for many friends, including many children who are present. This can be done in a very polite, quiet way, setting an example by your own life.

Everything a mother eats, drinks, worries about, or fears will have an effect on the fetus inside her. Even when the child inside is still tiny, everything is in it. If the mother is not aware of the nature of interbeing, she may cause damage to both herself and her child at the same time. If she drinks alcohol, she will destroy, to some extent, the brain cells in her fetus. Modern research has proven this.

When we eat mindfully we are in close touch with the food. The food we eat comes to us from nature, from living beings, and from the cosmos. To touch it with our mindfulness is to show our gratitude. Eating in mindfulness can be a great joy. We pick up our food with our fork, look at it for a second before putting it into our mouth, and then chew it carefully and mindfully, at least fifty times. If we practice this, we will be in touch with the entire cosmos.

Being in touch also means knowing whether toxins are present in the food. We can recognize food as healthy or not thanks to our mindfulness. Before eating, members of a family can practice breathing in and out and looking at the food on the table. One person can pronounce the name of each dish, "potatoes," "salad," and so on. Calling something by its name helps us touch it deeply and see its true nature. At the same time, mindfulness reveals to us the presence or absence of toxins in each dish. Children enjoy doing this if we show them how.

Mindful eating is a good education. If you practice this way for some time, you will find that you will eat more carefully, and your practice of mindful eating will be an example for others. It is an art to eat in a way that brings mindfulness into our life.

We can have a careful diet for our body, and we can also have a careful diet for our consciousness, our mental health. We need to refrain from ingesting the kinds of intellectual "food" that bring toxins into our consciousness. We know that smoking cigarettes is not good for our health. We have worked hard to get the manufacturers to print a line on a pack of cigarettes: WARNING: SMOKING MAY BE HAZARDOUS TO YOUR HEALTH. That is a strong statement, but it was necessary because advertisements to promote smoking are very convincing. They give young people the idea that if they don't smoke, they are not really alive. These advertisements link smoking with nature, springtime, expensive cars, beautiful men and women, and high standards of living. One could believe that if you don't smoke or drink alcohol, you will not have any happiness at all in this life. This kind of advertising is dangerous; it penetrates into our unconscious. There are so many wonderful and healthy things to eat and drink. We have to show how this kind of propaganda misleads people.

Sometimes we don't need to eat or drink as much as we do, but it has become a kind of addiction. We feel so lonely. Loneliness is one of the afflictions of modern life. It is similar to the Third and Fourth Mindfulness Trainings—we feel lonely, so we engage in conversation, or even in a sexual relationship, hoping that the feeling of loneliness will go away. Drinking and eating can also be the result of loneliness. You want to drink or overeat in order to forget your loneliness, but what you eat may bring

toxins into your body. When you are lonely, you open the re-
frigerator, watch TV, read magazines or novels, or pick up the
telephone to talk. But unmindful consumption always makes
things worse.

The toxins around us can be overwhelming. There is so much
violence, hatred, and fear in the media that surrounds us. If we
spend one hour looking at a violent film, we will water the seeds
of violence, hatred, and fear in us. We do that, and we let our
children do that, too. Therefore we should have a family meet-
ing to discuss an intelligent policy concerning television
watching. We may have to label our TV sets the same way we
have labeled cigarettes: WARNING: WATCHING TELEVI-
SION CAN BE HAZARDOUS TO YOUR HEALTH. That is the
truth. We do not have to destroy our television set; we only
have to use it with wisdom and mindfulness.

Because we are lonely, we want to have conversations, but
our conversations can also bring about a lot of toxins. From
time to time, after speaking with someone, we feel paralyzed by
what we have just heard. Mindfulness will allow us to stop having the kinds of conversations that bring us more toxins.

I propose a three-part practice to detoxify ourselves. First,
look deeply into your body and your consciousness and identify the kinds of toxins that are already in you. We each have to
be our own doctor not only for our bodies, but also for our
minds. After we identify these toxins, we can try to expel them.
One way is to drink a lot of water. Another is to practice massage, to encourage the blood to come to the spot where the toxins are, so the blood can wash them away. A third is to breathe
deeply air that is fresh and clean. This brings more oxygen into
the blood and helps it expel the toxins in our bodies. There are

mechanisms in our bodies that try to neutralize and expel these substances, but our bodies may be too weak to do the job by themselves. While doing these things, we have to stop ingesting more toxins.

At the same time, we look into our consciousness to see what kinds of toxins are already in there. We have a lot of anger, despair, fear, hatred, craving, and jealousy—all these things were described by the Buddha as poisons. The Buddha spoke of the three basic poisons as anger, hatred, and delusion. There are many more than that, and we have to recognize their presence in us. Our happiness depends on our ability to transform them. We have not practiced, and so we have been carried away by our unmindful life-styles. The quality of our life depends very much on the amount of peace and joy that can be found in our bodies and consciousness. If there are too many poisons in our bodies and consciousness, the peace and joy in us will not be strong enough to make us happy. So the first step is to identify and recognize the poisons that are already in us.

The second step of the practice is to be mindful of what we are ingesting into our bodies and consciousness. Ask yourself: "What kind of toxins am I putting into my body today? What films am I watching today? What book am I reading? What magazine am I looking at? What kind of conversations am I having?" Try to recognize the toxins.

The third part of the practice is to prescribe for yourself a kind of diet. You can say to yourself: "Aware of the fact that there are many toxins in my body and consciousness, aware of the fact that I am ingesting this and that toxin into my body and consciousness every day, making myself sick and causing suffering to my beloved ones, I am determined to prescribe for myself a proper diet. I vow to ingest only items that preserve well-being, peace, and joy in my body and my consciousness. I am determined not to ingest more toxins into my body and consciousness. Therefore, I will refrain from ingesting into my body and consciousness these things, and I will make a list of them."

We know that there are many items that are nutritious, healthy, and delightful that we can consume every day. When we refrain from drinking alcohol, there are so many delicious and wholesome alternatives: fruit juices, teas, mineral waters. We don't have to deprive ourselves of the joys of living, not at all. There are many beautiful, informative, and entertaining programs on television. There are many excellent books and magazines to read. There are many wonderful people and many healthy subjects to talk about. By vowing to consume only items that preserve our well-being, peace, and joy, and the well-being, peace, and joy of our family and society, we need not deprive ourselves of the joys of living. Practicing this third exercise brings us deep peace and joy.

Practicing a diet is the essence of this mindfulness training. Wars and bombs are the products of our consciousness individually and collectively. Our collective consciousness has so much violence, fear, craving, and hatred in it, it can manifest in wars and bombs. The bombs are the product of our fear. Because others have powerful bombs, we try to make bombs even more powerful. Then the other nations hear that we have powerful bombs, and they try to make even more powerful bombs. Removing the bombs is not enough. Even if we could transport all the bombs to a distant planet, we would still not be safe, because the roots of the wars and the bombs are still intact in our collective consciousness. Transforming the toxins in our collective consciousness is the true way to uproot war.

When we hear of a brutal act of violence, of the torturing of prisoners by U.S. soldiers in Iraq, for example, many of us feel bewildered by how a person could do such a thing. But it is not the perpetrator's problem alone. Their act was the manifestation of our collective consciousness. That person is not the only one who is violent and full of hatred and fear. Most of us are like that. There is so much violence around us.

Every morning, when going to work, a police officer says, "I have to be careful or I may be killed. I will be unable to return to my family." A police officer practices fear every day, and because of that, he may do things that are quite unwise. Sometimes there is no real danger, but because he suspects he may be shot, he takes his gun and shoots first. He may shoot a child playing with a toy gun. Because society is like this, police officers are like that. "This is, because that is. This is like this, because that is like that." A violent society creates violent police officers. A fearful society creates fearful soldiers. The problem is never "a few rotten apples." We have to change the society from its roots, which is our collective consciousness, where the root-energies of fear, anger, greed, and hatred lie.

We cannot abolish war with angry demonstrations. We have to practice a diet for ourselves, our families, and our society. We have to do it with everyone else. In order to have healthy TV programs, we have to work with artists, writers, filmmakers, lawyers, and legislators. We have to step up the struggle. Meditation should not be a drug to make us oblivious to our real problems. It should produce awareness in us, and also in our families and in our society. Enlightenment has to be collective for us to achieve results. We have to stop the kinds of consuming that poison our collective consciousness.

I do not see any other way than the practice of these bodhisattva mindfulness trainings. We have to practice them as a society in order to produce the dramatic changes we need. To practice as a society will be possible only if each of us vows to practice as a bodhisattva. The problem is great. It concerns our survival and the survival of our species and our planet. It is not a matter of enjoying one glass of wine. If you stop drinking your glass of wine, you do it for the whole society.

The Fifth Mindfulness Training is exactly like the first one. When you practice non-killing and you know how to protect the lives of even small animals, you realize that eating less meat has do with the practice of the mindfulness training. If you are not able to stop eating meat entirely, at least make an effort to reduce eating meat. If you reduce eating meat and drinking alcohol by fifty percent, you will already be performing a miracle; that alone can solve the problem of hunger in the Third World. Practicing the mindfulness trainings is to make progress every day. That is why during the mindfulness trainings recitation ceremony, we always answer the question of whether we have made an effort to study and practice the mindfulness training by deep breathing. That is the best answer. Deep breathing means that I have made some effort, but I can do better.

No one can practice the mindfulness trainings perfectly, including the Buddha. The vegetarian dishes that were offered to him were not entirely vegetarian. Boiled vegetables contain dead bacteria. We cannot practice the First Mindfulness Training or any of the mindfulness trainings perfectly. But because of the real danger in our society, because alcoholism and drug addictions have destroyed so many families, we have lived in a way that will eradicate or at least lessen that kind of damage.

Some people come to Plum Village already struggling with alcohol and drug addictions and we encourage them to practice mindfulness and meditation to help them with their struggles. But I think the best thing we can offer to young people is the Fifth Mindfulness Training, to prevent someone from becoming involved with drugs in the first place. Parents especially need to know what spiritual food to give their children. So often, children feel spiritually starved by the wholly materialistic outlook of their parents. The parents are unable to transmit to the children the values of their spiritual heritage, and so the children try to find fulfillment in drugs. Drugs seem to be the only solution when teachers and parents are spiritually barren. Young people need to touch the feeling of deep-seated well-being within themselves without having to take drugs, and it is the task of educators to help them find spiritual nourishment and well-being. But if educators have not yet discovered for themselves a source of spiritual nourishment, how can they demonstrate to young people how that nourishment may be found?

The Fifth Mindfulness Training tells us to find wholesome, spiritual nourishment, not only for ourselves but also for our children and future generations. Wholesome, spiritual nourishment can be found in the moon, the spring blossoms, or the eyes of a child. The most basic meditation practices of becoming aware of our bodies, our minds, and our world can lead us into a far more rich and fulfilling state than drugs could ever do. We can celebrate the joys that are available in the simplest pleasures.

Consuming mindfully is the intelligent way to stop ingesting toxins into our consciousness and prevent the malaise from becoming overwhelming. Learning the art of touching and ingesting refreshing, nourishing, and healing elements is the way to restore our balance and transform the pain and loneliness that are already in us. To do this, we have to practice together. The practice of mindful consuming should become a national policy. It should be considered true peace education. Parents, teachers, educators, physicians, therapists, lawyers, novelists, reporters, filmmakers, economists, and legislators have to practice together. There must be ways of organizing this kind of practice.

The practice of mindfulness helps us be aware of what is going on. Once we are able to see deeply the suffering and the roots of the suffering, we will be motivated to act, to practice. The energy we need is not fear or anger; it is the energy of understanding and compassion. There is no need to blame or condemn. Those who are destroying themselves, their families, and their society by intoxicating themselves are not doing it intentionally. Their pain and loneliness are overwhelming, and they want to escape. They need to be helped, not punished. Only understanding and compassion on a collective level can liberate us. The practice of the Five Mindfulness Trainings is the practice of mindfulness and compassion. For a future to be possible for our children and their children, we have to practice.

# The Three Jewels

*I take refuge in the Buddha,*
*the one who shows me the way in this life.*

*I take refuge in the Dharma,*
*the way of understanding and love.*

*I take refuge in the Sangha,*
*the community that lives in harmony and awareness.*

IN THE BUDDHIST TRADITION, whenever you formally vow to study, practice, and observe the Five Mindfulness Trainings, you also take refuge in the Three Jewels—Buddha, Dharma, and Sangha. The Buddha is mindfulness itself; the Dharma is the way of understanding and love; and the Sangha is the community that supports our practice. The Three Jewels, *triratna*, are made of the same elements. Practicing the Five Mindfulness Trainings is a concrete expression of our appreciation and trust in these Three Jewels. Practicing the Five Mindfulness Trainings is to have faith in the path of mindfulness, understanding, and compassion, because the Five Mindfulness Trainings are made of these three elements.

When we were in our mother's womb, we felt secure—protected from heat, cold, hunger, and other adversities. Although we were not yet aware in the way we are now, we knew somehow that this was a safe place. The moment we were born and came into contact with adversity, we began to cry, and since that time we have yearned for the security of our mother's womb.

We live in a world that is impermanent and filled with suffering, and we feel insecure. We desire permanence, but everything is changing. We desire an absolute identity, but there are no permanent entities, not even the one we call our "self." To seek for refuge means, first of all, to look for a place that is safe, secure, and permanent, something we can rely on for a long time. We want a place like Heaven, where a strong, stable figure like God the Father will protect us, and we will not have to worry about anything. But Heaven is in the future.

In Asian literature, some poets expressed the belief that they lived in a safe, happy place before being exiled to Earth, and when they died, they would be able to return to that state of bliss and happiness. Other Asians believed that they were gods in previous lives but, because of mistakes they made, they were exiled on Earth. If they performed meritorious deeds in this life, they believed they would be able to return to that safe place. The wish to take refuge is a universal desire to return to a place where we are safe and secure. In Vietnamese, the words for "to take refuge" are literally, "to go back and rely on."

But how can we feel safe now? Things are impermanent. If a kernel of corn is not impermanent, it will never grow into an ear of corn. If your daughter is not impermanent, she will never grow up into a beautiful young lady. If dictatorships are not impermanent, there is no hope of replacing them. We need impermanence and we should be happy to say, "Long live impermanence, so that life can be possible." Still, in the depths of our being, we yearn for permanence.

In Buddhism there are two kinds of practice, devotional and transformational. To practice devotion is to rely primarily on the power of another, who may be a buddha or a god. To practice transformation is to rely more on yourself and the path you are following. To be devoted to the Dharma is different from practicing the Dharma. When you say, "I take refuge in the Dharma," you may be showing your faith in it, but that is not the same as practicing the Dharma. To say "I want to become a doctor" is an expression of the determination to practice medicine. But to become a doctor, you have to spend seven or eight years studying and practicing medicine. When you say, "I take refuge in the Buddha, the Dharma, and the Sangha," this may be only the willingness to practice. It is not because you make this statement that you are already practicing. You enter the path of transformation when you begin to practice the things you pronounce.

But pronouncing words does have an effect. When you say, "I am determined to study medicine," that already has an impact on your life, even before you apply to medical school. You want to do it, and because of your willingness and desire, you will find a way to go to school. When you say, "I take refuge in the Dharma," you are expressing confidence in the Dharma. You see the Dharma as something wholesome, and you want to orient yourself toward it. That is devotion. When you study and apply the Dharma in your daily life, that is transformational practice. In every religion, there is the distinction between devotional practice and transformational practice.

Many Buddhists recite the Three Refuges as a devotional practice. We need faith and confidence in order to practice. In Buddhism, faith and confidence are linked to each other, and sometimes mean the same thing. However, blind faith is not encouraged. We have to see, touch, experiment with, and verify things before we truly believe in them. The Buddha, the Dharma, and the Sangha are things we can touch. They are not matters of speculation. The Buddha is a human being who lived in history. His life and teachings are known to us. We can use our time, energy, and intelligence to get in touch with the Buddha. Real faith and confidence arise from being in touch, not just from someone saying something we are expected to believe.

We can go directly to the Dharma. The Dharma exists in written form, in the tradition, and in the practice of people. Where people are practicing the Dharma, we can see the fruit of their practice. The Dharma is also something concrete that we can touch, experiment with, and verify, and this brings about real faith and confidence.

The Sangha is a community that practices the Dharma. A good Sangha expresses the Dharma. When we see a practicing Sangha that reveals some degree of peace, calm, happiness, and transformation, faith and confidence arise in us. Imagine I am someone who has not had anything to believe in for a long time. I have had no peace. But suddenly I see a community of people who have transformed themselves to some extent through the practice. Now I have faith and confidence, and that brings me some degree of peace. Devotion in Buddhism is not accepting a theory without touching the reality.

Many laypeople in Buddhist countries recite, "I take refuge

in the Buddha, I take refuge in the Dharma, I take refuge in the Sangha," but they rely on monks and nuns to practice for them. They support the practicing Sangha by offering food, shelter, and other things that help the Sangha succeed in its practice of the Dharma. They feel that the practice of one person living in real happiness brings happiness to many people. This is devotional practice. For these people, to pronounce the words, "I take refuge in the Buddha, I take refuge in the Dharma, I take refuge in the Sangha" is already enough to have peace and joy. But in North America and Europe, laypeople want to practice transformation. The vipassana meditation community in the West, for example, is comprised of people who practice—they do not just rely on monks and nuns—and there are many lay teachers.

When the layman Anathapindika was about to die, the Venerable Sariputra, knowing how much Anathapindika loved the Buddha and had faith in the Dharma and Sangha, invited him to meditate on the Three Jewels. Anathapindika felt great relief and was then invited by Sariputra to meditate on other subjects usually reserved for monks and nuns. These experiences watered Anathapindika's seeds of peace and joy.

A few months before he passed away, the Buddha taught his disciples to take refuge in themselves. "Bhikkhus, be an island unto yourself. Don't take refuge in anything else. Take refuge in the Dharma. Use the Dharma as your lamp. Use the Dharma as your island." He prepared very well for his passing away.

The Buddha said, "My physical body will not be here, but my Dharma body, *dharmakaya*, will be with you forever. If you want to take refuge in my Dharma body, you can do that at any time." In later Buddhist history, the Dharma body became the spirit or the soul of the Buddha, i.e., the true Buddha that is available throughout time. If we know how to touch the dharmakaya, it is available to us, our children, and their children at any time. To see clearly that the physical body is not as important as the Dharma body was a comfort to the Buddha's disciples. Today our society has so much suffering and danger in it, like a strong current trying to pull us into the ocean of sorrow. To protect ourselves, we too can practice being islands unto ourselves.

Every Buddha and every practitioner has his or her Sangha body, *sanghakaya*. A Buddha can only be a Buddha when the Dharma is in him or her. Without the Dharma, someone cannot be called a Buddha. The Buddha and the Dharma are two, but one. A Buddha cannot be without the Dharma. The Dharma cannot be without the Buddha. A Sangha is a community that practices the Dharma. If there is no Sangha, who is practicing the Dharma? The Dharma is not tangible if there are no practitioners. If you want the Dharma to be practiced, you need a Sangha. Therefore the Sangha contains the Buddha and the Dharma.

The Buddha, the Dharma, and the Sangha inter-are. Each jewel contains the other two. When you take refuge in one, you take refuge in all three. When you have confidence and trust in the Sangha and practice with the Sangha, you are expressing your confidence in the Buddha and the Dharma. It is crucial to practice the mindfulness trainings with a Sangha, a community of practice. You need a Sangha to support you in the practice. A true Sangha always possesses in its heart the Buddha and the Dharma.

Devotional practice in Buddhism is based on what can be seen, heard, and touched. If we are not in touch with the physical Buddha, we cannot be in touch with the Dharma body of the Buddha, or the Sangha body of the Buddha. Because we have information about the life of the physical Buddha, our devotion is well-grounded. This is also true in Christianity. Jesus is someone we can touch. Information about his life and teachings is available.

In the Anguttara Nikaya, the Buddha said that when you are agitated, afraid, lacking in confidence, or weak, if you practice taking refuge in the Buddha, the Dharma, and the Sangha, your fear and instability will dissolve. He told the story of the fighting between Sakra, the king of the gods, and the *asuras*. Sakra commanded his troop of *devas*, or heavenly soldiers, to fly his flag of seven jewels.* Every time they lacked confidence in fighting the asuras, if they looked at the flag, they would find the strength and confidence needed. This is natural. If you have confidence in your commander, you will fight well as a soldier. When you believe in a good cause, you have the courage to stand your ground. The Buddha used this example to talk about taking refuge. When you have doubts, weakness, or agitation, if you focus your attention on the Buddha, the Dharma, and the Sangha, you become firm again. This is the fruit of practicing the Three Refuges in its devotional form.

But taking refuge can also be a transformational practice. What makes the Buddha a Buddha is enlightenment, the living Dharma, which is the fruit of practice. The Tripitaka, the three baskets of the teachings, is the Dharma, but not the living Dharma. The Dharma as audiotapes, videotapes, or books is not the living Dharma. The living Dharma must be observed in a

---

* Asuras are gods or spirits who are easily angered and are prone to fighting. Devas are celestial beings who inhabit the heavenly realms.

Fully Enlightened One, a Buddha, or in those not yet fully enlightened who are really practicing. The essence of the Dharma is enlightenment, which is to understand, to be aware.

The practice of mindfulness is the key to enlightenment. When you become aware of something, you begin to have enlightenment. When you drink a cup of water and are aware that you are drinking a cup of water deeply with your whole being, enlightenment in its initial form is there. To be enlightened is to be enlightened on something. I am enlightened on the fact that I am drinking a cup of water. I can get joy, peace, and happiness just because of that enlightenment. When you look at the blue sky and are aware of the blue sky, the blue sky becomes real, and you become real. That is enlightenment, and enlightenment brings about true life and true happiness.

The substance of a Buddha is mindfulness. Every time you go back to your breath and practice breathing deeply in mindfulness, you are a living Buddha. When you are not sure what to do, go back to your breath—breathe in and out consciously—and take refuge in mindfulness. The best thing to do in moments of difficulty is to go back to yourself and dwell in mindfulness. When you are in bed and unable to sleep, the best thing to do is go back to your breathing. You are safe and happy knowing that no matter what happens, you are doing the best thing you can do. Taking refuge in the Buddha, not as a devotion, but as true practice, is very comforting. Every time you feel confused, angry, lost, agitated, or afraid, you always have a place which you can return to. Mindfulness of breathing is your own island. It is very safe. "Be an island unto yourself" means that you should know how to go back to yourself in case of danger, instability, or loss. This practice of taking refuge is very concrete. When you go back to your breath—breathing in and out deeply—and light the lamp of mindfulness in yourself, you are safe. In that state of mindfulness, you are truly yourself. The lamp is already lit, and the possibility of seeing things more clearly is great.

Suppose you are on a boat crossing the ocean. If you get caught in a storm, stay calm and don't panic. To accomplish that, you go back to your breathing and be yourself. Because you are calm, truly your own island, you will know what to do and what not to do. If you do not, the boat may capsize. We destroy ourselves by doing things we ought not do. Take refuge in mindfulness, and you will see things more clearly and know what to do to improve the situation. This is a very deep practice. Mindfulness brings about concentration, and concentration brings about insight and wisdom. This is the safest place to take refuge now, and not just in the future.

The safety and stability that your island can provide depend on your practice. Everything—baking a cake, building a house, playing volleyball—depends on your practice. If you are a beginner who practices going back to your island of self every time you feel upset, you will enjoy some mindfulness, concentration, and peace. The moment you begin to practice, Buddha, Dharma, and Sangha are available to you to some extent. But this cannot be compared to the mindfulness, concentration, and peace of someone who has been practicing for a long time. At first, your Buddha may be just some information you have read about him, the Dharma just what you have heard from a friend, and the Sangha a community you have touched once or twice. As you continue to practice, the Buddha, the Dharma, and the Sangha will reveal themselves more fully to you. Your

Buddha is not identical to my Buddha. They are both Buddha, but the degree to which that is revealed depends on our practice.

The Buddha taught that there are three fundamental characteristics of life: impermanence, non-self, and nirvana. A teaching that contradicts any of these Three Seals is not an authentic Buddhist teaching. If we don't know that everything is impermanent, we will suffer. If we don't know that everything is without a self, without an absolute identity, we will suffer. But there is the possibility of not suffering, thanks to nirvana. Nirvana is the absence of delusion concerning the nature of impermanence and non-self. When you look deeply into the true nature of reality, if you realize the nature of impermanence and non-self, you are free from suffering. You may think that nirvana is the opposite of impermanence and non-self. But if you continue to practice, you will see that nirvana is found in the world of impermanence and non-self.

Visualize the ocean with countless waves on it. On the one hand, we see that all waves begin with birth and end with death. They can be big or small, high or low. If we look into their nature, we see that the waves are impermanent and without a self. But if we look more deeply, we see that the waves are also water. The moment the wave realizes that it is water, all fear of death, impermanence, and non-self will disappear. Water is, at the same time, wave and not-wave, yet waves are made only of water. Notions like big or small, high or low, beginning or end can be applied to waves, but water is free of all these distinctions. Nirvana can be found in the heart of life, which is characterized by birth and death. That is why, if you practice taking refuge deeply, one day you will know that you are free from birth and death. You are free from the kinds of dangers that have been assaulting you. When you are able to see that, you will be able to construct a boat to ride on the waves of birth and death, smiling, like a bodhisattva. You will no longer fear birth and death. You do not have to abandon this world and seek some faraway paradise in order to be free.

The Buddha rarely talked about nirvana, the unconditioned, because he knew that if he talked about it, we would spend all of our time talking about it and not practicing. But he did make a few rare statements concerning nirvana. Let us read this statement from the Nibbana Sutta, Udana 8.3 of the Pali Canon: "Verily, there is an unborn, unoriginated, uncreated, unformed. If there were not this unborn, unoriginated, uncreated, unformed, then an escape from the world of the born, the originated, the created, and the formed, would not be possible." Early Buddhism did not have the ontological flavor we see in later Buddhism. The Buddha dealt more with the phenomenal world. His teaching was very practical. Theologians spend a lot of ink, time, and breath talking about God. This is exactly what the Buddha did not want his disciples to do, because he wanted them to have time to practice *samatha* (stopping, calming), *vipassana* (looking deeply), taking refuge in the Three Jewels, the Five Mindfulness Trainings, and so on.

In other places, the teaching of the Buddha reveals to us the unconditioned. For instance, he says, "When conditions are sufficient, the eyes are perceived by us as existing. When conditions are no longer sufficient, the eyes are not perceived by us as existing. The eyes have not come from somewhere in space. The eyes will not go anywhere in space." The idea of coming, going, being, and nonbeing are representations and concepts to be extinguished. If there is something that you cannot talk about, it is best not to talk about it. Wittgenstein said the same thing in his *Tractatus Logico-Philosophicus:* "Concerning that which cannot be talked about, we should not say anything." We cannot talk about it, but we can experience it. We can experience the non-born, non-dying, non-beginning, non-ending, because it is reality itself. The way to experience it is to abandon our habit of perceiving everything through concepts and representations. Theologians have spent thousands of years talking about God as one representation. This is called ontotheology, and it is talking about what we should not talk about.

The Buddha that we experience here and now is mindfulness. Mindfulness is a mental formation like any other mental formation. It has a seed in our individual consciousness and in our collective consciousness. It is a precious gem buried deep in the Earth for us to discover and explore. When we unearth it, we can transform the whole situation. This is the coming of a Buddha—not from nothingness, not from nonbeing, but from a Buddha seed, Buddha nature. The Buddha nature is, first of all, mindfulness.

The practice of mindfulness is the practice of bringing the Buddha into life in the present moment. It is the real Buddha. That is why the Buddha is sometimes described in Mahayana Buddhism as the Tathagata ("he or she who has come from suchness, from reality-as-it-is"). Suchness cannot be described with words or concepts. Nirvana, the absolute truth, reality-as-it-is, is the object of our true perception and insight. But an object of perception always includes the subject of perception. With mindfulness, we can see the nature of reality clearly. Mindfulness, with the support of concentration, conscious

breathing, and looking deeply, becomes a power that can penetrate deeply and directly into the heart of things. It is not speculation, using concepts and words, but direct looking. Finally,
the true nature of reality will be revealed to us as suchness.
Reality-as-it-is cannot be described by words and concepts, but
can be penetrated by prajña, true understanding. In each of us,
the seed of mindfulness can be described as the womb of the
Buddha, *tathagatagarbha*.

We are all mothers of the Buddha, because all of us are pregnant with a Buddha. If we know how to take care of our baby
Buddha, one day this Buddha will be revealed to us. That is why
at Plum Village we bow to each other as a sign of greeting, saying silently, "A lotus for you, a Buddha-to-be." We see the other
person as the mother of a future Buddha. In each of us is a
Buddha-embryo, the seed of mindfulness, and this is what we
need to take refuge in in our daily lives. The Buddha is said to
have ten names, and the first, Tathagata, means "one who has
arrived from suchness, remains in suchness, and will return to
suchness." Like the Buddha, we have come from suchness, remain in suchness, and will return to suchness. We have nowhere
to go, have come from nowhere, and are going nowhere.

It is not just absolute reality that cannot be talked about. It
is not just the Buddha who is like that. We are also like that.
Nothing can be conceived or talked about. A glass of orange
juice itself is absolute reality. We cannot talk about orange juice
to someone who has not tasted it. No matter what we say, the
other person will not have the true experience of orange juice.
The only way is to drink it. It is like a turtle telling a fish about
life on dry land. You cannot describe dry land to a fish. He could
never understand how one might be able to breathe without

water. Things cannot be described by concepts and words. They can only be encountered by direct experience.

When Wittgenstein said, "That which cannot be talked about should not be talked about," you might think there are things that we can talk about and things we cannot. But in fact, nothing can be talked about, perceived, or described by representation. If you talk about things you have not experienced, you are wasting your time and other people's time as well. As you continue the practice of taking refuge, you will see this more and more clearly, and you will save a lot of time, paper, and publishing enterprises, and have more time to enjoy your tea and live your daily life in mindfulness.

The second name of the Buddha is Arhat, meaning "one who is worthy of our support and respect." The third is Samyaksambuddha, "one whose knowledge and practice are perfect." The fourth is Vidyacaranasampana, "one who is equipped with knowledge and practice." The fifth is Sugata, "one who is welcome." The sixth is Lokavida, "one who knows the world well." The seventh is Anutta-apurusadamyasarathi, meaning "unsurpassed leader of people to be trained and taught." The eighth is Sastadeva-manussana, "teacher of gods and humans." The ninth is Buddha, "enlightened one." The tenth is Bhagavat, "blessed one." Every time we take refuge in the Buddha, we take refuge in the one who has these attributes. When we take refuge in our mindfulness, we take refuge in the seed of these attributes in us.

In Mahayana Buddhism, tathagatagarbha is equivalent to the dharmakaya, the body of the Dharma. When we talk about suchness or nirvana, we are talking about that which should not be talked about. The Buddha mostly refrained from talking about these things, but he did, from time to time, offer a hint by talking about other things. The teaching of no coming, no going, no being, no nonbeing was already very clear in early Buddhism. In Mahayana Buddhism, these ideas became fully developed, sometimes a little overdeveloped. We should not indulge ourselves too much in things like that. We should preserve the practical nature of the Buddhadharma. Otherwise we will become philosophers and not practitioners.

When I practice taking refuge in my breathing, I say, "Breathing in, I go back to myself. Breathing out, I take refuge in my own island. Mindfulness is the Buddha that illuminates my path." I practice mindful breathing as a practice of taking refuge.

We live in a world of impermanence and non-self, a world in which many waves are trying to carry us away. We practice dwelling in our mindfulness as our own island. Mindfulness is the Buddha in person. It is also the Dharma and the Sangha. Practicing mindful breathing, we shine the light of mindfulness upon the five *skandhas*, or aggregates of being, namely, form, feelings, perceptions, mental formations, and consciousness in us. There is a Sangha of five elements inside us, and there may be a lack of harmony among them. Suffering results from conflicts between skandhas. Mindfulness of breathing can calm the conflicts and reestablish harmony in us. The fruits of this practice are peace and joy.

When you look deeply, the nature of non-birth, non-death, non-coming, non-going are revealed to you, and the fear that you may lose this or that will disappear. You do not have to abandon this world. You do not have to go to heaven for refuge. You do not have to wait for the future to have refuge. You take refuge here and now. The depth of your refuge depends on your practice. Buddha, Dharma, and Sangha are always available. The womb of the Tathagata is always there. We only need to go back there in order to be safe.

In the Greek Orthodox church, theologians talk about "apophatic theology," or "negative theology." "Apophatic" is from the Greek word *apophasis*, which means "denying." You say that God is not this, God is not that, until you get rid of all your concepts of God. The second century Buddhist philosopher Nagarjuna developed a similar dialectic to remove our ideas concerning reality. He did not describe reality, because reality is what it is and cannot be described. When Zen Buddhists talk about killing the Buddha, they mean that the Buddha-concept should be killed in order for the real Buddha to be directly experienced.

The idea of the Trinity in the Orthodox Christian church is quite deep and sophisticated. Sometimes our friends in the Orthodox church say that the Trinity is their social program. They begin with the Holy Spirit and the Son. The Father may be more difficult to touch, think about, or perceive. The Father belongs to the realm of inexpressibility and should be kept in that mystical realm. But it is possible to touch the Son and the Holy Spirit. Similarly, in Buddhism we talk about practicing with the Dharma and Sangha, and later on, touching nirvana, "the Tathagata-womb."

The Holy Spirit creates the Son, so the Son can show us the way to the Father. I told a Christian monk, "It is much safer to begin with the Holy Spirit. You have the capacity to recognize the presence of the Holy Spirit whenever and wherever It manifests Itself. It is the presence of mindfulness, understanding, and love, the energy that animates not only Jesus but all of us. That energy helps us recognize the Living Christ and touch the ground of being that is God the Father. In Buddhism, the Holy Spirit is called mindfulness, awakening, prajña, maitri, and karuna. Touching this energy, you touch the Buddha and nirvana."

The theology of the death of God, the idea of atheistic and secular Christianity is very much in the same spirit. You depend on the person of Jesus Christ and his teaching and practice. This is very intelligent and pragmatic. If you begin with the idea of God, you may get stuck. In the Greek Orthodox church, the idea of deification, that a person is a microcosm of God, is very inspiring. It was already evident in the fourth century, and it is very much like the Asian tradition that states that "the body of a human being is a mini-cosmos." God has made humans so that humans can become God. A human being is a mini-God, a micro-theos. This is close to the idea that the Tathagata is in every one of us. We are all pregnant with a Buddha. According to the theology of deification, humans are made in order to participate in the divinity of God, not just as separate creations. Deification is made not only of the spirit, but of the body of a human also. According to the teaching of the Trinity in the Orthodox church, the Father is the source of divinity who engenders the Son. With the "Word" (Greek: *logos*), he brings about the spirit that is alive in the Son. This is comparable to the nondual nature of the Buddha, Dharma, and Sangha.

The most important thing in a multireligious dialogue is for each side to tell the other side how they practice. If we come together for five or ten days, we should be able to share with each other how we live our daily lives, how we practice taking refuge, how we pray, meditate, and so on. To me the Five Mind-fulness Trainings are the practice of mindfulness. The Three Refuges are also the practice of mindfulness. "I take refuge in the Sangha" is very much a practice, and not a devotion.

Mystery in Christianity sometimes is described as darkness. By the third or fourth century in the Greek Orthodox church, the idea of darkness was already there, and it has become a source for Christian mysticism. Darkness means that you cannot know it; you cannot see it clearly with your intellect; it is mysterious. When Victor Hugo lost his daughter Leopoldine, he complained that "Man sees only one side of things, the other side is plunged into the night of the frightening mystery." In Buddhism, mystery is described in terms of light. In the Avatamsaka Sutra, the Buddha is light. If you are struck by one of the beams, you will get enlightened. In the Avatamsaka Sutra, the Buddha was giving a talk in the form of Vairocana Buddha, that is, the Dharmakaya Buddha, and humans, gods, Buddhas, bodhisattvas, carpenters, kings, policemen—everyone in the assembly experienced bliss because they had been touched by the beams of light emanating from the Buddha. In Buddhism, the word *avidya* means the lack of wisdom, insight, and light. *Vidya*, understanding, is made of light. Everything that is mystical and wonderful is on the side of the light, not on the side of the darkness. Although it cannot be grasped by conceptual knowledge, it is light.

In a short story, Alphonse Daudet talks about a shepherd on a mountain who made the Sign of the Cross when he saw a shooting star. The popular belief is that at the moment you see a shooting star, one soul is entering heaven. Making the Sign of the Cross is a form of taking refuge in the Trinity: the Father,

Son, and the Holy Spirit. When you believe that something is the embodiment of evil, you hold out a cross to chase it away. In popular Buddhism, when people see something they think of as unwholesome, they also invoke the name of Buddha. That is a practice of devotion. When there is light, darkness disappears.

But if we learn the principle of nonduality, our understanding changes. One practice of mindfulness is to recite this verse as we turn on the light in a room:

> Forgetfulness is the darkness,
> mindfulness is the light.
> I bring awareness,
> to shine upon all life.

We may understand this as a kind of fight between light and darkness, but in reality, it is an embrace. Mindfulness, if practiced continuously, will be strong enough to embrace your fear or anger and transform them. Reciting a mantra is not like holding out a cross to chase away evil. It should be practiced in a nonviolent, nondualistic way.

In Christianity, taking refuge is expressed by the body of Jesus. To some people, the image of the cross expresses too much suffering. There must be ways to represent the Father, Son, and Holy Spirit as peace, joy, and happiness other than through the image of the cross. Some people say that they feel more peaceful when they see the image of the Buddha sitting and smiling. To look at a person being crucified for two thousand years may be too much. I like very much that the practice be manifested in a body, but what about an image of Jesus holding a lamb? That may be more appealing. When we practice sitting meditation, it is expressed in the body. When we practice prostrations, it is also an act of taking refuge. All the five elements are all focused in one direction, the pole of mindfulness.

In Christianity, the Eucharist is an act of taking refuge in Jesus, God. Not much is said about experiencing deeply the Dharma and the Sangha. Without the Sangha, the community in the church, and without the eating of bread and drinking of wine in awareness, there could be no Jesus. The Sangha has been important in Christianity. People never celebrate a Eucharist on their own but come together as a Sangha. In the early church, the expression "we are all one body" was much used. But the hierarchy of the church became oppressive and the Sangha weakened as a result.

In Buddhist practice, we stress the Sangha. If you leave the Sangha, it is said to be like the tiger leaving his mountain. A tiger that comes to the lowlands can be caught by humans and killed. A practitioner without a Sangha can lose her practice.

The traditional Sangha community is made up of four communities—monks, nuns, laymen, and laywomen. I would add the supportive elements that are not human, like trees, cushions, rocks, water, and birds. A pebble, a leaf, a dahlia, a tree, a bird, and a path, are all preaching the Saddharmapundarika Sutra, if we know how to listen. In the Pure Land (Sukhavativyuha) Sutra, it is said that when the wind blows through the trees, we can hear the teaching of the Four Establishments of Mindfulness, the Eightfold Path, the Four Powers, and so on. The whole cosmos is preaching and practicing the Buddhadharma. If we are attentive, we can touch that Sangha.

Everyone who wants to practice needs a Sangha. We have to

set up small Sanghas around us to support us in the practice. Without a Sangha, when we become exhausted, we will have no means to nourish ourselves. By creating a small Sangha, you can find the greater Sangha around and inside us.

The practice of taking refuge can be done every day, several times a day. Every time you feel unwell, agitated, sad, afraid, or worried—these are times to go back to your island of mindfulness. If you practice going back to your island when you are not experiencing difficulty, when you do have a problem, it will be easier and more enjoyable. Do not wait until you are hit by a wave in order to go back to your island. Practice going back to your island by living mindfully every moment of your life. If the practice becomes a habit, when the difficult moments arrive, it will be natural and easy to do. Walking, breathing, sitting, eating in silence, and drinking tea in mindfulness are all practices of taking refuge. Every mindfulness practice contains all the other practices. If you just practice taking refuge, you are also practicing the Eightfold Path, the Four Establishments of Mindfulness, and everything else. One Dharma door contains all Dharma doors.

Taking refuge is not a matter of belief. It is very grounded in our experience. You know that you have the seed of mindfulness in you. You have the island within yourself. It is not a metaphysical question. Your in-breath and out-breath are available; your seed of mindfulness is always there. Taking refuge is a matter of daily practice. In Vietnamese Buddhist temples, we use the words *công phu*, which mean "daily practice." A good student or teacher always goes back and takes refuge in the mindfulness of breathing when he is angry or worried.

When we receive bad news and we feel shaken by it, the best

thing to do at that moment is to take refuge. In the West, when you have to tell someone bad news, you ask him to sit down. Sitting down is good, because you are afraid he will faint. But you can also ask him to breathe in and out to be calm and solid. Even good news can make someone faint. If you hear that you have just won ten million dollars in the lottery, you might have a heart attack and die.

It is not always easy to practice taking refuge in this way. Because of our tendency to believe in a permanent self, we need to practice deeply enough to realize the nature of no coming, no going. Otherwise, we will stick to the idea that before we were born, we were somewhere, and when we die, we go somewhere. Because we don't know where we are going, we feel afraid. The teaching of the Pure Land assures people that if they practice well now, they will be reborn in the Pure Land of Amida Buddha. There are other Pure Lands as well, such as the Abhirati of Aksobhya. Many Buddhists want to be reborn in Tushita Heaven to be with the Buddha Maitreya, and when the time comes for him to be reborn on Earth, they want to come with him.

To be reborn in the Pure Land, you have to practice recollection of the Buddha. During your daily life, you can invoke the name of the Buddha and focus your attention on the Buddha. This is a form of taking refuge. You practice either by visualizing the Buddha, with his thirty-two beautiful marks, or by invoking his name. The name of the Buddha can bring about the good qualities of the Buddha. During the time you practice, you dwell in that kind of refuge of the Buddha. You are close to him, to the island. You water the seed of Buddhahood—mindfulness and goodness—in yourself. Later you learn from your teacher that the Pure Land is in your heart. These are gradual steps toward the teaching of no coming and no going. Many people need a place to go before they realize that they do not have to go anywhere.

We have to remember that Pure Lands are impermanent. In Christianity, the Kingdom of God is the place you will go for eternity. But in Buddhism, the Pure Land is a kind of university where you will practice with a teacher for a while, graduate, and then come back here again. An enlightened being named Amida Buddha asked those who have an affinity with the practice to come with him and practice, so that they can graduate one day and become fully enlightened persons. If you realize that the Pure Land is in your heart, as in the teaching of the Avatamsaka Sutra, you don't need a faraway place or time to set up a Pure Land. You can set up a Sangha, a mini-Pure Land, right now at home.

Here is another way of phrasing how we can take refuge in the Three Jewels:

*Going back, taking refuge in the Buddha in myself, I vow to realize the Great Way in order to give rise to the highest mind.* The highest mind is *bodhicitta,* the intention or vow to practice and help countless living beings until you attain full enlightenment. There are those who practice just to relieve their own suffering and don't think about the suffering of others. That is not the highest mind.

*Going back, taking refuge in the Dharma in myself, I vow to attain understanding and wisdom as immense as the ocean.* The living Dharma can be touched only through the manifestation of a Buddha, a Sangha, or a good practitioner.

*Going back, taking refuge in the Sangha in myself, I vow, together with all beings, to help build a Sangha without obstacles.* If you are motivated by the desire to set up a small Sangha in order to practice and to make friends happy with the practice, you are practicing the Third Refuge. If you suffer because you do not have confidence in your practice and feel on the verge of leaving the Sangha, that is unfortunate. If you feel unhappy in the Sangha, if you find your Sangha too difficult to handle, it is best to make the effort to continue. We do not need a perfect Sangha. An imperfect one is good enough. We can do our best to transform ourselves into a positive element of the Sangha and encourage the rest of the group to be supported by our effort.

The Three Refuges are a very deep practice. Here is another way of phrasing these simple words so that young people can understand them easily:

> I take refuge in the Buddha,
> the one who shows me the way in this life.
>
> I take refuge in the Dharma,
> the way of understanding and love.
>
> I take refuge in the Sangha,
> the community that lives in harmony and awareness.

We know that the Three Jewels inter-are. Without a Dharma and a Sangha, a Buddha is not a Buddha. Even Buddhas-to-be need a Dharma body and a Sangha body. These are up to us to build. Our Dharma body should be a living body and not just a set of dogmas or ideas. Our Sangha body should be a living community, and not just a dream of looking for land or looking for like-minded people. The best way is to manifest it here and now, to make this Sangha a living Sangha today, to make the Dharma that we have learned the living Dharma today. If we are determined, everything will come together. Learning from the Sutra on Knowing the Better Way to Live Alone, we practice in the present moment to enjoy the present moment, which is our Sangha here and now.

A Buddha like Shakyamuni can be seen through his Dharma body and his Sangha body. When you touch his Dharma body or his Sangha body, you touch him. We should not complain that we were born 2,500 years too late and therefore cannot touch him. We are touching him. We are touching his Dharma body and his Sangha body right now. All of us Buddhas-to-be need to express ourselves in our Dharma body and in our Sangha body. When someone says something that provokes us, we can smile and return to our breathing, and she will have a chance to touch our Dharma body. When we act mindfully and compassionately, our Dharma is the living Dharma. Every time we have some difficulty or frustration, if we go back to our breathing and dwell in our island of mindfulness, everyone can touch our living Dharma. When we have a group of friends who support each other in the practice of the Dharma, every time someone joins us for a cup of tea, they touch our Sangha body.

The Buddha said that his body of teachings would remain with his students, but that it was up to them to make it last. If we don't practice, there will be only books and tapes, but if we practice, the Dharma body will be a living Dharma. "Dharmakaya" later acquired the meaning "soul of the Buddha," "spirit of the Buddha," "true Buddha," "ground of the Buddha." It developed an ontological flavor, "ground of all beings," "ground of all enlightenment." Finally, it became something equivalent to "suchness," "nirvana," and "tathagatagarbha." That is a natural development. The Dharma is the door that opens to all of these meanings. We only need to be concerned about how much time we spend talking about these things.

Dharmakaya is the Buddha in substance. Sometimes we call it Vairocana, the ontological Buddha, the Buddha as the base, the embodiment of the Dharma, always shining, always enlightening trees, grass, birds, human beings, and so on, always emitting light. It is that Buddha who is preaching the Avatamsaka Sutra now and not just 2,500 years ago. Those who get in touch with Vairocana do not need Shakyamuni. Shakyamuni is just a beam of rays sent by Vairocana Buddha. Shakyamuni is the nirmanakaya, the transformation body, a spark sent forth by the center of the fire, a beam sent by the sun. We don't need to worry if one beam ceases to be apparent. The sun is always there. The dharmakaya is always there. If you cannot listen directly to Shakyamuni, if you are open enough, you can listen to Vairocana. In addition to Shakyamuni, many transformation Buddhas are preaching. The trees, birds, violet bamboos, and yellow chrysanthemums are all preaching the same Dharma that Shakyamuni taught 2,500 years ago. We can be in touch with the nirmanakaya, through either

The first body is the dharmakaya, the second body is the *sambhogakaya*, and the third body is the nirmanakaya. The sambhogakaya is the body of bliss. You can get in touch with that body because the Buddha fulfilled his wish of full enlightenment. Mindfulness is the base of understanding, compassion, peace, and happiness. When we breathe in and out and become aware of the blue sky, we enjoy it. When we take our tea in mindfulness, we are in touch. Peace, joy, and happiness are the fruits of mindfulness. The Buddha who practices mindfulness has immeasurable peace, joy, and happiness, and we can touch this body of enjoyment. Every time you touch something in harmony, something that shines, you touch the sambhogakaya of the Buddha. That is the rewards body, the body of enjoyment, symbolizing the peace and happiness of the Buddha, the fruit of his practice.

The rewards body can be described in two ways. The first is self-enjoyment. The second is the enjoyment experienced by others. When you practice mindfulness, you enjoy within you the fruit of the practice. Those around you also enjoy your happiness and the fruits of your practice. When someone is happy and peaceful, that happiness and peace radiates around him for others to enjoy. If you practice well, you will be able to send many sambhogakayas into the world in order to help relieve the suffering of living beings. One person has the capacity of transforming many living beings if she knows how to explore the seed of enlightenment within her.

One day when I was in an airplane, I had this thought: If the pilot were to announce that the plane was about to crash, what would I do? It was clear to me that I would practice mindful breathing and smiling. That is the best thing I could do in that moment. And if, down there, you knew that I was practicing breathing and smiling during that difficult moment, you would have confidence in yourself. It is essential that we do not wait until such a critical moment in order to begin the practice.

I always practice mindful breathing during takeoffs and landings. That doesn't mean that in between I don't do this, but rather that I never fail to do it at these times. It's not because I'm afraid, but it has become a habit. I travel so much. I also have the habit of practicing walking meditation at airports. I always try to leave for the airport early, so that I will not have to rush when I am there. Everyone is rushing, but I know it is possible to be yourself and practice walking meditation even there.

The Three Jewels and the Five Mindfulness Trainings are both teachings about the practice of mindfulness. The Three Jewels embrace every teaching and are the foundation of every practice. This is the kind of practice you can gauge. You will be able to see the progress you are making. Your trust and faith in the Three Jewels will be strengthened every day.

# Afterword:
## Happiness Comes from the Heart

JACK KORNFIELD

Conscious conduct or virtue means acting harmoniously and with care toward the life around us. For spiritual practice to develop, it is essential that we establish a basis of moral conduct in our lives. If we are engaged in actions that cause pain and conflict to ourselves and others, it is impossible for the mind to become settled, collected, and focused in meditation; it is impossible for the heart to open. In a mind grounded in unselfishness and truth, concentration and wisdom develop easily.

The Buddha outlined five areas of basic morality that lead to a conscious life. These mindfulness trainings are given to all students who wish to follow the path of mindfulness. They are not given as absolute commandments; rather, they are practical guidelines to help us live in a more harmonious way and develop peace and power of mind. As we work with them, we discover that they are universal trainings that apply to any culture, in any time. They are a part of basic mindfulness practice and can be cultivated in our spiritual life.

The First Mindfulness Training is to refrain from killing. It means honoring all life, not acting out of hatred or aversion in such a way as to cause harm to any living creature. We work to develop a reverence and caring for life in all its forms. In the

Eightfold Path this is called one aspect of right action. Even though it sounds obvious, we still manage to forget it. There was a cartoon in the *New Yorker* some years ago during the hunting season. One deer turns to the other and says, "Why don't they thin their own goddamn herds?" We get into formulating excuses: "Well, there are too many deer." As we become more conscious and connected with life, it becomes clear that we shouldn't harm others, because it hurts us to kill. And they don't like it; even the tiniest creatures don't wish to die. So in practicing this training we learn to stop creating pain for others and pain for ourselves.

The Second Mindfulness Training asks us to refrain from stealing, meaning not to take what is not ours. Not to steal is called basic non-harming. We need to let go of being greedy and not take too much. More positively, it means to use things with sensitivity and care, to develop our sense of sharing this life, this planet. To live, we need plants, we need animals, and we need insects. This whole world has to share its resources. It is a boat of a certain size with so many beings living on it. We're connected with the bees and the insects and the earthworms. If there weren't earthworms to aerate the soil, and if there weren't bees to pollinate the crops, we'd starve. We need bees, we need insects. We're all interwoven. If we can learn to love the Earth, we can be happy whatever we do, with a happiness born of contentment. This is the source of genuine ecology. It's a source of world peace when we see that we're not separate from the Earth, but that we all come out of it and are connected with one another. From this sense of connectedness we can commit ourselves to share, to live a life of helpfulness and generosity for the world. To cultivate generosity directly is another fundamental part of living a spiritual life. Like the mindfulness trainings and like our inner meditations, generosity can actually be practiced. With practice, its spirit forms our actions, and our hearts will grow stronger and lighter. It can lead us to new levels of letting go and great happiness. The Buddha emphasized the importance of generosity when he said, "If you knew what I know about the power of giving, you would not let a single meal pass without sharing it in some way."

Traditionally there are described three kinds of giving, and we are encouraged to begin developing generosity at whatever level we find it arising in our heart. At first we find tentative giving. This is where we take an object and think, "Well, I'm probably not going to use this anyway. Maybe I should give it away. No, I should save it for next year. No, I'll give it away." Even this level is positive. It creates some joy for us and it helps someone else. It's a sharing and connecting.

The next level of generosity to discover is friendly giving. It's like relating to a brother or sister. "Please share what I have; enjoy this as I do." Sharing openly of our time, our energy, the things we have, feels even better. It's lovely to do. The fact is that we do not need a lot of possessions to be happy. It is our relationship to this changing life that determines our happiness or sorrow. Happiness comes from the heart.

The third level of giving is kingly or queenly giving. It's where we take something—our time or our energy or an object that is the best we have—and give it to someone happily and say, "Please, would you enjoy this too." We give to the other person and take our joy in that sharing. This level of giving is a beautiful thing to learn.

As we start to learn to be more generous, to give more of our time, our energy, our goods, our money, we can find a way to do it not just to fit a self-image or please an external authority, but because it is a source of genuine happiness in our lives. Of course this doesn't mean giving everything away. That would be excessive, because we have to be compassionate and care for ourselves as well. Yet to understand the power of practicing this kind of openness is very special. It is a privilege to be able to bring this generosity into our lives.

The Third Mindfulness Training, to refrain from sexual misconduct, reminds us not to act out of sexual desire in such a way as to cause harm to another. It requires that we be responsible and honest in sexual relations. Sexual energy is very powerful. In these times of rapidly changing relationships and sexual values, we are asked to become conscious of our use of this energy. If we associate this energy in our lives with grasping and greed, exploitation and compulsion, we will perform actions that bring harm to ourselves and others, such as adultery. There is great suffering consequent to these actions and great joy in the simplicity that comes in their absence. The spirit of this training asks us to look at the motivation behind our actions. To pay attention in this way allows us, as laypeople, to discover how sexuality can be connected to the heart and how it can be an expression of love, caring, and genuine intimacy. We have almost all been fools at some time in our sexual lives, and we have also used sex to try to touch what is beautiful, to touch another person deeply. Conscious sexuality is an essential part of living a mindful life.

The Fourth Mindfulness Training of conscious conduct is to refrain from false speech. The Eightfold Path calls this right speech. Don't lie, it says. Speak only what is true and useful;

speak wisely, responsibly, and appropriately. Right speech really poses a question. It asks us to be aware of how we actually use the energy of our words. We spend much of our lives talking and analyzing and discussing and gossiping and planning. Most of this talk is not very conscious or aware. It is possible to use speech to become awake. We can be mindful of what we are doing when we speak, of what the motivation is and how we are feeling. We can also be mindful in listening. We can align our speech to the principles of what is truthful and what is most kind or helpful. In practicing mindfulness we can begin to understand and discover the power of speech.

Once a master was called to heal a sick child with a few words of prayer. A skeptic in the crowd observed it all and expressed doubts about such a superficial way of healing. The master turned to him and said, "You know nothing of these matters; you are an ignorant fool!" The skeptic became very upset. He turned red and shook with anger. Before he could gather himself to reply, however, the master spoke again, asking, "When one word has the power to make you hot and angry, why should not another word have the power to heal?"

Our speech is powerful. It can be destructive and enlightening, idle gossip or compassionate communication. We are asked to be mindful and let our speech come from the heart. When we speak what is true and helpful, people are attracted to us. To be mindful and honest makes our minds quieter and more open, our hearts happier and more peaceful.

To refrain from the heedless use of intoxicants is the Fifth Mindfulness Training. It means to avoid taking intoxicants to the point of making the mind cloudy and to devote our lives to developing clarity and alertness. We have just one mind, so we

must take care of it. In our country, there are millions of alcoholics and others who have abused drugs. Their unconscious-
ness and their fearful use of intoxicants have caused great pain
to themselves, their families, and all those they touch. To live
consciously is not easy—it means we often must face fears and
pains that challenge the heart. Abuse of intoxicants is clearly
not the way.

I would like to offer some exercises that can help us use the
Five Mindfulness Trainings to cultivate and strengthen mindfulness. It is best to choose one of these exercises and work with
it meticulously for a week. Then examine the results and choose
another for a subsequent week. These practices can help us understand and find ways to work with each training.

1. *Refraining from killing: reverence for life.* Undertake for one
   week to purposefully bring no harm in thought, word, or
   deed to any living creature. Particularly, become aware of
   any living beings in your world (people, animals, even
   plants) whom you ignore, and cultivate a sense of care and
   reverence for them too.

2. *Refraining from stealing: care with material goods.* Undertake
   for one week to act on every single thought of generosity
   that arises spontaneously in your heart.

3. *Refraining from sexual misconduct: conscious sexuality.* Undertake for one week to observe meticulously how often sexual feelings arise in your consciousness. Each time, note
   what particular mind states you find associated with them,
   such as love, tension, compulsion, caring, loneliness, desire for communication, greed, pleasure, aggression, and
   so forth.

4. *Refraining from false speech: speech from the heart.* Undertake for one week not to gossip (positively or negatively) or speak about anyone you know who is not present with you (any third party).

5. *Refraining from intoxicants to the point of heedlessness.* Undertake for one week or one month to refrain from all intoxicants and addictive substances (such as wine, marijuana, even cigarettes and/or caffeine if you wish). Observe the impulses to use these, and become aware of what is going on in the heart and mind at the time of those impulses.

To enter the human realm, to establish a ground for spiritual life, requires that we bring awareness to all the actions in our world, to our use of intoxicants, our speech, to all of our actions. Establishing a virtuous and harmonious relationship to the world brings ease and lightness to the heart and steadfast clarity to the mind. A foundation of virtue brings great happiness and liberation in itself and is the precondition for wise meditation. With it we can be conscious and not waste the extraordinary opportunity of a human birth, the opportunity to grow in compassion and true understanding in our life.

# Appendix 1
## Frequently Asked Questions
### SISTER CHÂN KHÔNG

HERE ARE a number of responses we have offered to those who love the beauty and goodness of the mindfulness trainings, but hesitate to receive them formally:

**Question: I was born a Christian. Do I have to abandon my faith to receive the Five Mindfulness Trainings formally?**
Response: A tree that has no root cannot survive; you cannot grow well spiritually if you have no roots. You should not abandon your root religion. Please practice mindfulness as a base with the Five Mindfulness Trainings as guidelines. With mindfulness you can look deeply into your root tradition and discover many wonderful jewels in it. You might rediscover guidelines within your own tradition that you can share with both Christian and non-Christian friends.

**Question: When I took the Five Mindfulness Trainings with another Buddhist teacher, the wording was not stated as clearly as it is in the mindfulness trainings of Thich Nhat Hanh. Can I take them again?**
Response: Yes. The Five Mindfulness Trainings are from the Buddha. Your root teacher continues to be your root teacher.

The new wording of the Five Mindfulness Trainings offered by Thây is to help you practice the teachings of the Buddha well. Your root teacher will be pleased if you renew your vows in this way. He or she will always be your first teacher. Thây Nhat Hanh will be your second, or third, or fourth teacher. We can have many teachers to enrich ourselves.

**Question: I want to practice the Five Mindfulness Trainings, but why is it necessary to take refuge in the Three Jewels?**
Response: Without a strong belief in these three precious jewels, you really cannot practice the Five Mindfulness Trainings. "I take refuge in the Buddha" means that I strongly believe in my ability to become enlightened, to transform my difficulties and be free of all suffering, and to be a source of joy and peace for myself and others. "Buddha" means the buddha in me, the potential for awakening in me. I know that Shakyamuni Buddha is my teacher. I also know that he is not a god.

"I take refuge in the Dharma" means that I believe in the practice of mindfulness, which brings understanding and love. I believe in the method that Shakyamuni Buddha offered from his own experience to me, so that I can realize the path that leads to freedom from suffering.

"I take refuge in the Sangha" means that I believe in the collective wisdom of a group of friends who vow to practice the same method as I do on our path of liberation. We need each other for support and to share our experiences of practice so that our perceptions will grow closer to reality and our actions will become more harmonious. We support each other on the path of realization and, in doing so collectively, our efforts benefit ourselves and all beings.

Without faith and confidence in the Three Jewels, it is difficult to practice the Five Mindfulness Trainings well.

**Question: Can I take only one, two, three, or four of the Five Mindfulness Trainings?**
Response: The Buddha said yes, you can. If you practice even one mindfulness training deeply, you will find that you are also keeping the other four, even without making a formal promise to do so. The Five Mindfulness Trainings are very much interconnected.

**Question: If I take the First Mindfulness Training, does it mean I have to become a vegetarian?**
Response: Thây Nhat Hanh asks us to practice mindfulness deeply every time we eat or drink. If we do so, we may find that our appetite for meat and fish begins to diminish. The important thing is to be aware of what we consume. I have met people who cannot be vegetarian because of medical reasons, but who respect life more than many vegetarians. Some vegetarians are too extreme, and are unkind to those who cannot give up meat-eating. I am more comfortable with a meat-eater than an extremist vegetarian who is filled with self-righteousness.

**Question: Many of my friends, including myself, have two or three sexual partners. How do you suggest that I keep the Third Mindfulness Training?**
Response: When you do two or three things at the same time, like eating your dinner, watching television, and having a conversation with friends at the dinner table, you do not do any of the three things deeply. You cannot truly taste and enjoy each

morsel of food that your beloved one prepared for you. You cannot give your full attention to the television program, and you will be unable to listen carefully to what your friends are saying. It is even more difficult if you have several sexual partners at the same time. Please examine this deeply. None of your relations will be profound. Ask your heart whether you are really happy. It may seem all right now, but are you certain that you are not causing suffering to yourself or your partners? A superficial, non-committed relationship never leads to real happiness or peace.

**Question (from a teenager): In my school, everyone my age is sexually active. Why shouldn't I be? If I don't act like them, my friends will think I'm odd.**
Response: A sexual relationship is a very deep act for mutual peace and the preservation of the species. Acting in a superficial way damages our body and mind. When our mind is not ready for such a deep act, our feelings, perceptions, and understanding towards that friend will not be profound enough, and a sexual act will increase the risk of destroying the friendship. You may think that a sexual act is just like any other act you do for fun or enjoyment, but many young people have told me that they realize afterwards that it was a mistake. Sex is deeper than other acts. The hurt from having sex in a non-committed way can be profound, and the wound may remain unhealed for many years. Birth control has nothing to do with these mental wounds. Many teenagers report that they had no joy in their life, no desire to live after receiving a mental wound from having a sexual relationship they were not ready for. Usually we only share our very deep secrets with those with whom we have

had a long experience of appreciation and trust. This is also true with our bodies. We shouldn't share our bodies with someone with whom we do not intend to have a long-term commitment.

**Question: Can I take the Fifth Mindfulness Training, and still drink an occasional glass of wine or beer with dinner?**
Response: Thây Nhat Hanh advises us not to drink any alcohol, if possible. If you still have a strong inclination to drink, please do so mindfully. Look deeply into the conditions of your liver, your heart, and the fact that humankind is wasting a lot of grain and fruit making alcohol instead of feeding other humans. Meditating in this way will lead us to feeling uncomfortable when drinking any amount of alcohol.

If you are not ready to stop drinking entirely, please take the first four mindfulness trainings and try to drink mindfully until you are ready to stop. Thây Nhat Hanh advises those who take the Fifth Mindfulness Training not to drink at all, even one glass of wine or beer a week. French authorities advise their citizens that one glass of alcohol is okay, but that three is saying hello to the damage that an accident can cause. But how can you have a second or third glass if you haven't had the first?

Under normal conditions, we may drink one or two glasses of wine from time to time. But in moments of despair, we might have five, six, or seven glasses in order to forget our sorrows. This can lead to alcohol abuse. A lovely grandmother on a retreat in England asked this question, and I told her, "You are a moderate drinker, but are you sure all your sons, daughters, and grandchildren are like you? If during one or two moments of despair they gradually drink more and more and become alcoholic and destroy themselves physically and mentally, who would be responsible? Haven't you participated partly in that process? If you keep the Fifth Mindfulness Training now, you may be the torch for the future generations of your grandchildren. You keep the mindfulness trainings as a bodhisattva and not as an order that you are forced to obey."

**Question: If I break a training, to whom should I confess?**
Response: Confess to your own Buddha. The best way to practice is with a group of friends, even just one or two. Making efforts to follow this path of beauty, you can share with them your successes and failures. Reciting the mindfulness trainings regularly, with the group, helps very much. During the Mindfulness Trainings recitation, following the reading of each training, this question is asked, "Have you made an effort to study and practice it during the past two weeks?" If you have broken the training, you can say, silently, to yourself, "I am deeply aware that I was not mindful and have broken this mindfulness training. From now on, I will try to do better." Don't feel too guilty. Your habit energy is still strong. The fact that you are aware of your negative act will decrease that habit energy each time you recite the training, and soon your habit will be transformed.

**Question: In tending a garden, I often find it necessary to kill certain "pests"—worms, insects, and rodents that destroy the garden. Is this against the First Mindfulness Training? Also, I don't know how to deal with infestations of ants, cockroaches, and other household "pests." How does a practicing Buddhist deal with these problems?**
Response: Even when we boil a kettle of water, we must be

aware that we are killing many microorganisms in the process. Our effort is not to kill, so we try various methods to do the least harm to all living creatures. For example, in gardening, we learn about how to grow certain plants next to our cultivated flowers and vegetables that repel insects, worms, and rodents. We try our best not to use harmful pesticides, but use organic ones that don't kill the animals if possible. Likewise, we try to keep out ants and cockroaches by harmless means—keeping food out of their reach, using organic repellents, or just being patient. If finally, we deem it necessary to kill these creatures, it is most important to be aware of the fact that we are indeed killing them. With mindfulness, we continue to make efforts not to do harm (even as we are aware that harm has been done). Nonviolence can never be absolute. But we can continue to do our best to minimize the harm we cause and to maximize our appreciation and reverence for all life—people, animals, plants, and minerals.

I would like to tell you about a friend named James, who has suffered tremendously. As a child of five, he was beaten by his mother and pushed down two flights of stairs on his bicycle. He recalled how all the acts of violence from his mother followed a period when she was drinking. One day, he was beaten until his left eye was badly swollen and blue. At school, when his teacher asked why his eye was swollen, he told the truth. His teacher called home, and his mother denied that she had beaten her son. At forty-two, James still cries like a five-year-old when he recalls, "He believed her, and I was punished for lying. I continued to tell the truth, and they punished me."

His mother sent him to live with his grandmother, who used drugs and alcohol. When he was seven, she began to abuse him sexually and beat him, especially when she was drunk. Other unbelievable acts of violence were inflicted on him as a result of her use of drugs or alcohol. He ran away from his grandmother's home and went back to his mother, but she too began abusing him sexually. So finally he saved enough money to escape to his father. When he called him to say he was in town and wished to live with him, his father panicked and sent him back home. When he was seventeen, his father encouraged him to join the army and go to Vietnam. Before he said good-bye, his father gave him a slap on the back and said, "The army will make a man out of you, son." James cried again.

One afternoon, in Plum Village, James described how overwhelmed with despair he was looking at all the young Vietnamese boys and girls, who reminded him of those he had killed in Vietnam. After several days and nights of gunfire from his helicopter, he would get out of his plane and discover human bodies stacked on each other like logs in rows for several hundred meters. "How could I bring these bodies back to life?" His friends tried to comfort him, saying, "That's what war is, James, you couldn't help it." James can tell you how, looking back over his life, the roots of war began in the violence of his parents' divorce and his parents' alcoholism and sexual abuse.

I have been an assistant of Thây Nhat Hanh in leading many retreats on mindfulness practice for Vietnamese and Western friends since 1983. I always encourage people to tell their difficulties to Thây, so he can help them transform their long-lasting pain. But as Thây cannot see everyone, I have listened to many people's pain. The story of James is one of dozens of similar stories from war veterans and others. So many had fathers or mothers who were alcoholics, and so many came from broken families. At first, I thought this was an American problem, but later, while assisting Thây on retreats in England, Germany, Switzerland, Italy, and France, I heard the same sad stories there. So much suffering comes from the fact that people drink too much, are irresponsible with their sexual conduct, lie, cause suffering to others with their unmindful speech, or spread news they are not sure is true. So many people were raised by drunken adults, or adults with polluted minds who abused children, because the adults themselves had been victims during their own childhoods. I realized that adults who terrorize their children were themselves victims.

A way out of the suffering is for us to join with a group of people who are joyful and who try to practice going in the direction of goodness, beauty, and truth. The people in the group must sincerely look at their own weaknesses, smile at them, and consider the weaknesses as part of the compost to be transformed into flowers. Today there are so many polluted minds and such an atmosphere of violence and abuse. We need to find a way out. The Five Mindfulness Trainings represent a beautiful road that leads to awakening. Even if we ourselves were not abused as children or have no problems with alcohol abuse, sexual irresponsibility, etc., we can help many others by formally receiving these trainings and practicing them. We can be an example for many people, and help lead them in the direction of joy and peace.

To practice the Five Mindfulness Trainings, it is helpful to remember these points:

- Mindfulness is the ground of all the trainings. We would not need to keep any particular training if we were capable of being mindful twenty-four hours a day. But since that is not the case, we need to practice the Five Mindfulness Trainings or their equivalent as a guideline.

- The wording of the Five Mindfulness Trainings presented by Thây Nhat Hanh in this book is in the spirit offered by Shakyamuni Buddha, updated to respond to the needs and difficulties of people of our day.

- No one can keep the mindfulness trainings totally. Even the Buddha himself could not do this. When boiling vegetables to eat, we kill microorganisms in the water, or when taking an antibiotic, we kill microorganisms in our intestines. If we live mindfully, it is good enough to gently move in the direction of acting without violence.

- The direction of the Five Mindfulness Trainings is the direction of beauty, goodness, and truth. To transform our collective consciousness into beauty, goodness, and truth, we move in that direction, as we would go in the direction of the sun. We cannot climb onto the sun, and we don't need to. To move in that direction is good enough.

- As we try our best to move in that direction, knowing that no one is able to live up to his best, we need a group of friends with whom we can practice regularly and share our experiences of living the mindfulness trainings. As we encounter difficulties, says Thây Nhat Hanh, we must practice with a Sangha and regularly recite the trainings together to remind and inspire each other and try to find ways out of the most difficult situations in our families and society. That is why Thây says that the ordination ceremony will be nullified if the ordinee does not recite the mindfulness trainings at least once every three months with his or her Sangha.

The situation of the world today is so violent and confused that for a future to be possible, not only individuals, but even nations need to take the Five Mindfulness Trainings.

# Appendix 2
## The Five Mindfulness Trainings Ceremonies

CEREMONY TO TRANSMIT THE THREE REFUGES,
TWO PROMISES, AND FIVE MINDFULNESS
TRAININGS

[THIS CEREMONY MUST BE PRESIDED OVER BY SOMEONE WHO HAS
RECEIVED THE FULL ORDINATION OF A MONK OR A NUN, OR A MEM-
BER OF THE COMMUNITY OF INTERBEING WHO HAS RECEIVED THE
TRANSMISSION OF THE LAMP AND IS A DHARMA TEACHER.]

1. OPENING THE CEREMONY

*Sitting Meditation* [12 MINUTES]

*Incense Offering*
In gratitude, we offer this incense
throughout space and time
to all Buddhas and Bodhisattvas.
May it be fragrant as Earth herself,
reflecting careful efforts, wholehearted awareness,
and the fruit of understanding slowly ripening.
May we and all beings
be companions of Buddhas and Bodhisattvas.
May we awaken from forgetfulness
and realize our true home.

*Touching the Earth*
*Opening Gatha*

The one who bows and the one who is bowed to
are both, by nature, empty.
Therefore the communication between them
is inexpressibly perfect.
Our practice center is the Net of Indra
reflecting all Buddhas everywhere.
And with my person in front of each Buddha,
I go with my whole life for refuge.

[BELL]


*Prostrations*

[TOUCH THE EARTH AT EACH SOUND OF THE BELL]

Offering light in the Ten Directions,
the Buddha, the Dharma, and the Sangha,
to whom we bow in gratitude.

[BELL]

Teaching and living the way of awareness
in the very midst of suffering and confusion,
Shakyamuni Buddha, the Fully Enlightened One,
to whom we bow in gratitude.

[BELL]

Cutting through ignorance, awakening our hearts and our
minds,
Manjushri, the Bodhisattva of Great Understanding,
to whom we bow in gratitude.

[BELL]

Working mindfully, working joyfully for the sake of all beings,
Samantabhadra, the Bodhisattva of Great Action,
to whom we bow in gratitude.
[BELL]

Listening deeply, serving beings in countless ways,
Avalokiteshvara, the Bodhisattva of Great Compassion,
to whom we bow in gratitude.
[BELL]

Fearless and persevering through realms of suffering and
darkness,
Kshitigarbha, the Bodhisattva of Great Aspiration,
to whom we bow in gratitude.
[BELL]

Seed of awakening and loving kindness
in children and all beings,
Maitreya, the Buddha to-be-born,
to whom we bow in gratitude.
[BELL]

Showing the way fearlessly and compassionately,
the stream of all our Ancestral Teachers,
to whom we bow in gratitude.
[BELL, BELL]

## 2. Opening Verse

[BELL, BELL, BELL]

Namo Tassa Bhagavato Arahato Samma Sambuddhassa
Namo Tassa Bhagavato Arahato Samma Sambuddhassa
Namo Tassa Bhagavato Arahato Samma Sambuddhassa

[BELL]

The Dharma is deep and lovely.
We now have a chance to see, study, and practice it.
We vow to realize its true meaning.

[BELL]

## 3. The Heart of Perfect Understanding

The Bodhisattva Avalokita,
while moving in the deep course of Perfect Understanding,
shed light on the Five Skandhas and found them equally
empty.
After this penetration, he overcame ill-being.

[BELL]

Listen, Shariputra,
form is emptiness, and emptiness is form.
Form is not other than emptiness, emptiness is not other than
form.
The same is true with feelings, perceptions, mental formations, and consciousness.

[BELL]

Listen, Shariputra,
all dharmas are marked with emptiness.
They are neither produced nor destroyed,

neither defiled nor immaculate,
neither increasing nor decreasing.
Therefore in emptiness there is neither form, nor feelings, nor
perceptions, nor mental formations, nor consciousness.
No eye, or ear, or nose, or tongue, or body, or mind.
No form, no sound, no smell, no taste, no touch, no object of
mind.
No realms of elements (from eyes to mind consciousness),
no interdependent origins and no extinction of them
(from ignorance to death and decay).
No ill-being, no cause of ill-being, no end of ill-being, and no
path.
No understanding and no attainment.
[BELL]

Because there is no attainment,
the bodhisattvas, grounded in Perfect Understanding,
find no obstacles for their minds.
Having no obstacles, they overcome fear,
liberating themselves forever from illusion, realizing perfect
nirvana.
All Buddhas in the past, present, and future,
thanks to this Perfect Understanding,
arrive at full, right, and universal enlightenment.
[BELL]

Therefore one should know
that Perfect Understanding is the highest mantra,
the unequaled mantra,
the destroyer of ill-being, the incorruptible truth.

A mantra of Prajñaparamita should therefore be proclaimed:

Gate gate paragate parasamgate bodhi svaha
Gate gate paragate parasamgate bodhi svaha
Gate gate paragate parasamgate bodhi svaha
[BELL]

## 4. SANGHAKARMAN PROCEDURE*

Sanghakarman Master: Has the entire community assembled?
Sangha Convener: The entire community has assembled.
Sanghakarman Master: Is there harmony in the community?*
Sangha Convener: Yes, there is harmony.
Sanghakarman Master: Why has the community assembled today?
Sangha Convener: The community has assembled to perform the Sanghakarman of transmitting the Three Refuges, Two Promises, and Five Mindfulness Trainings.
Sanghakarman Master: Noble community, today, [DATE], has been chosen as the day to transmit the Three Refuges, Two Promises, and Five Mindfulness Trainings. The community has assembled at the appointed time and is ready to transmit and receive the Three Refuges, Two Promises, and Five Mindfulness Trainings in an atmosphere of harmony. Thus, the transmission can proceed.
Is this statement clear and complete?

---

*The transmission of the Five Mindfulness Trainings should be done when the community is in harmony. The practice of Beginning Anew will help the community resolve conflicts.

Everyone: Clear and complete.
[REPEAT QUESTION AND ANSWER THREE TIMES]
[BELL]

## 5. INTRODUCTORY WORDS

Today the community has gathered to give spiritual support to our brothers and sisters [NAMES] who will go for refuge to the Three Jewels and make the vow to practice the Two Promises and Five Mindfulness Trainings. Will the entire community please enjoy your breathing and remain mindful when you hear the three sounds of the bell. The sound of the bell is the voice of the Buddha, bringing us back to our true selves.
[BELL, BELL, BELL]

## 6. TOUCHING THE EARTH IN GRATITUDE

Will our brothers and sisters who are receiving the promises and the mindfulness trainings please come forward with joined palms and stand before the Three Jewels? If there is anyone whose name was not read and who wishes to receive the Three Refuges, Two Promises, and Five Mindfulness Trainings, please stand up now and say your name clearly, then come forward before the Three Jewels.

Ordinees, on hearing the sound of the bell, after the recitation of each line, please touch the Earth one time.

In gratitude to our parents who have given us life,
we touch the Earth before the Three Jewels.
[BELL]

In gratitude to our teachers who show us how to love,
understand, and live in the present moment,
we touch the Earth before the Three Jewels.
[BELL]

In gratitude to our friends who guide us on the path
and support us in difficult moments,
we touch the Earth before the Three Jewels.
[BELL]

In gratitude to all species in the animal, plant, and mineral worlds,
who support our life and make our world beautiful,
we touch the Earth before the Three Jewels.
[BELL, BELL]

## 7. THE THREE REFUGES

Today the community has gathered to give support to those who will vow to go for refuge to the Three Jewels and receive and practice the Two Promises and Five Mindfulness Trainings. You have had the chance to learn about and observe the way of understanding and love that has been handed down to us by teachers over many centuries, and today you have made the decision to go for refuge to the Three Jewels and receive the Two Promises and Five Mindfulness Trainings.

To take refuge in the Three Jewels is to turn to the Buddha, the Dharma, and the Sangha for protection. The Buddha, the Dharma, and the Sangha are Three Precious Gems. To take refuge in the Buddha is to take refuge in the Awakened One who has the ability to show us the way in this life. To take refuge in the Dharma is to take refuge in the way of understanding, love, and compassion. To take refuge in the Sangha is to take refuge in a community that practices according to the path of understanding, love, and compassion and lives in an awakened way.

The Buddha, the Dharma, and the Sangha are present in every quarter of the universe as well as in every person and all other species. To go for refuge to the Buddha, the Dharma, and the Sangha also means to have confidence in our own ability to be awakened, to develop and manifest understanding and love in ourselves, and to practice the Way for ourselves and for our family, our community, and society. Will the brothers and sisters please repeat after me the Three Great Refuge Vows:

I take refuge in the Buddha,
the one who shows me the way in this life.
[BELL]
[ORDINEES TOUCH THE EARTH ONE TIME]

I take refuge in the Dharma,
the way of understanding and love.
BELL]
[ORDINEES TOUCH THE EARTH ONE TIME]

I take refuge in the Sangha,
the community that lives in harmony and awareness.
[BELL, BELL]
[ORDINEES TOUCH THE EARTH ONE TIME]

Brothers and Sisters, you have formally received the Three Refuges. Receiving them will enable you to see the Three Jewels in your own heart and bring them into your daily life. Today you have become students of the Awakened One and have made the vow to live an awakened life. Beginning from today you will apply your mind to learning about and practicing the way of understanding, love, and compassion, which means to nourish the ability to love and understand within yourselves. You will also go for refuge to your Sangha in order to learn and practice, and you will attend days and retreats of mindfulness and recitations of the trainings and other activities of your Sangha.

The transmitter of the Refuges to you is [NAME OF TRANSMITTER], and your Dharma name will be chosen by him (or her). You should take refuge in your teacher and your Sangha to learn and practice the path.

## 8. THE TWO PROMISES (FOR CHILDREN)

Young people, you have received the Three Refuges into your heart. Now you have become students of the Awakened Ones, and will live in an awakened way. Now you are going to receive the Two Promises that you will make with the Buddha-seed in yourself. These two promises will help you be aware of the suffering and the happiness of people, animals, plants, and minerals. You will be able to look after and preserve this planet Earth. Will the entire community please join the young people in repeating after me:

I vow to develop understanding
in order to life peacefully
with people, animals, plants, and minerals.

This is the First Promise. Do you promise to the Buddha-seed within you that you will do your best to practice it?
[BELL]

I vow to develop my compassion
in order to protect the lives
of people, animals, plants, and minerals.

This is the Second Promise. Do you promise to the Buddha-
seed within you that you will do your best to practice it?
[BELL]

Young students of the Enlightened One, understanding and
love are the two most important teachings of the Buddha. If we
try to be open and to understand the difficulties of other people, we will be able to love them and to live in harmony with
them. The same is true for animals, plants, and minerals. If we
cannot understand others then we cannot love. The Buddha
teaches us to look at living beings with the eyes of love and understanding. Please learn to practice this teaching.

Young people, upon hearing the sound of the bell, please
stand up and touch the Earth three times to the Three Jewels,
and then you can go back to your seat.
[BELL, BELL, BELL]
[THE YOUNG PEOPLE TOUCH THE EARTH]

### 9. READING THE TWO PROMISES CERTIFICATE
[THE TRANSMITTER READS THE CERTIFICATE ON WHICH IS
WRITTEN THE TWO PROMISES, THE DHARMA NAME OF THE
CHILD, AND THE NAME OF HIS OR HER TEACHER. THEN THE CER-
TIFICATE IS GIVEN TO THE YOUNG PERSON.]

Brothers and Sisters I will now read the Mindfulness Trainings
Certificate. When you hear your name, please come forward to
receive your certificate.

[THE YOUNG PEOPLE MAY NOW LEAVE THE HALL OR THEY MAY STAY TO LISTEN TO THE OTHER TRAININGS.]

## 10. TRANSMITTING THE FIVE MINDFULNESS TRAININGS

Brothers and Sisters, now is the time to transmit the Five Mindfulness Trainings. They have the capacity to protect life and make it beautiful. The Five Mindfulness Trainings encourage us in the direction of peace, joy, liberation, and awakening. They are the foundation for individual happiness and the happiness of the family and society. If we practice according to the Five Mindfulness Trainings, we are already on the path of a bodhisattva. The Five Mindfulness Trainings protect us and help us avoid making mistakes and creating suffering, fear, and despair. Practicing these trainings, we are able to build peace and happiness in ourselves and our family, and joy and peace in our society.

I will now recite the Five Mindfulness Trainings. Listen carefully with a calm and clear mind. Say, "Yes, I do" every time you see you have the capacity to receive, learn, and practice the mindfulness training read.

[BELL]

Sisters and Brothers, are you ready?
Ordinees: Yes, I am ready.


### The First Mindfulness Training

Aware of the suffering caused by the destruction of life, I am committed to cultivating compassion and learning ways to protect the lives of people, animals, plants, and minerals. I am determined not to kill, not to let others kill, and not to support any act of killing in the world, in my thinking, and in my way of life.

This is the first of the Five Mindfulness Trainings. Do you make the commitment to receive, study, and practice it?

Ordinees: Yes, I do.
[BELL]
[ORDINEES TOUCH THE EARTH ONE TIME]

*The Second Mindfulness Training*
Aware of the suffering caused by exploitation, social injustice, stealing, and oppression, I am committed to cultivating loving kindness and learning ways to work for the well-being of people, animals, plants, and minerals. I will practice generosity by sharing my time, energy, and material resources with those who are in real need. I am determined not to steal and not to possess anything that should belong to others. I will respect the property of others, but I will prevent others from profiting from human suffering or the suffering of other species on Earth.

This is the second of the Five Mindfulness Trainings. Do you make the commitment to receive, study, and practice it?

Ordinees: Yes, I do.
[BELL]
[ORDINEES TOUCH THE EARTH ONE TIME]

## The Third Mindfulness Training

Aware of the suffering caused by sexual misconduct, I am committed to cultivating responsibility and learning ways to protect the safety and integrity of individuals, couples, families, and society. I am determined not to engage in sexual relations without love and a long-term commitment. To preserve the happiness of myself and others, I am determined to respect my commitments and the commitments of others. I will do everything in my power to protect children from sexual abuse and to prevent couples and families from being broken by sexual misconduct.

This is the third of the Five Mindfulness Trainings. Do you make the commitment to receive, study, and practice it?

Ordinees: Yes, I do.

[BELL]

[ORDINEES TOUCH THE EARTH ONE TIME]

## The Fourth Mindfulness Training

Aware of the suffering caused by unmindful speech and the inability to listen to others, I am committed to cultivating loving speech and deep listening in order to bring joy and happiness to others and relieve others of their suffering. Knowing that words can create happiness or suffering, I am determined to speak truthfully, with words that inspire self-confidence, joy, and hope. I will not spread news that I do not know to be certain and will not criticize or condemn things of which I am not sure. I will refrain from uttering words that can cause division or discord, or that can cause the family or the community to break. I am determined to make all efforts to reconcile and re-solve all conflicts, however small.

This is the fourth of the Five Mindfulness Trainings. Do you make the commitment to receive, study, and practice it?

Ordinees: Yes, I do.
[BELL]
[ORDINEES TOUCH THE EARTH ONE TIME]

*The Fifth Mindfulness Training*
Aware of the suffering caused by unmindful consumption, I am committed to cultivating good health, both physical and men-tal, for myself, my family, and my society by practicing mindful eating, drinking, and consuming. I will ingest only items that preserve peace, well-being, and joy in my body, in my con-sciousness, and in the collective body and consciousness of my family and society. I am determined not to use alcohol or any other intoxicant or to ingest foods or other items that contain toxins, such as certain TV programs, magazines, books, films, and conversations. I am aware that to damage my body or my consciousness with these poisons is to betray my ancestors, my parents, my society, and future generations. I will work to transform violence, fear, anger, and confusion in myself and in society by practicing a diet for myself and for society. I under-stand that a proper diet is crucial for self-transformation and for the transformation of society.

This is the fifth of the Five Mindfulness Trainings. Do you make the commitment to receive, study, and practice it?

Ordinees: Yes, I do.
[BELL]
[ORDINEES TOUCH THE EARTH ONE TIME]

Brothers and Sisters, you have received the Five Mindfulness Trainings which are the foundation of happiness in the family and in society. They are the basis for the aspiration to help others. You should recite the trainings often, at least once a month, so that your understanding and practice of the Five Mindfulness Trainings can grow deeper every day.

A mindfulness trainings recitation ceremony can be organized in a practice center, with your local Sangha, or at home with friends. If you do not recite the trainings at least once in three months, you lose the transmission and today's ceremony will be nullified. Brothers and Sisters, as students of the Awakened One, you should be energetic in practicing the way the Buddha has taught to create peace and happiness for yourselves and all species. Upon hearing the sound of the bell, please stand up and bow deeply three times to show your gratitude to the Three Jewels.

[BELL, BELL, BELL]
[ORDINEES TOUCH THE EARTH THREE TIMES]

## 11. Reading the Mindfulness Trainings Certificate

[THE TRANSMITTER OF THE MINDFULNESS TRAININGS READS
THE CERTIFICATE ON WHICH IS WRITTEN THE DHARMA NAME OF
THE ORDINEE AND THE NAME OF HIS OR HER TEACHER. EACH
ORDINEE KNEELS WHILE LISTENING TO THE READING OF HIS OR
HER CERTIFICATE, AFTER WHICH THE CERTIFICATE IS GIVEN TO
HIM OR HER.]

Brothers and Sisters, I will now read the Mindfulness Trainings Certificate. When you hear your name, please come forward to receive your certificate.

## 12. Closing the Ceremony

Noble community, to lend spiritual support to our brothers and sisters who have been ordained, let us recite the closing verses in mindfulness:

## 13. The Three Refuges

I take refuge in the Buddha,
the one who shows me the way in this life.
I take refuge in the Dharma,
the way of understanding and of love.
I take refuge in the Sangha,
the community that lives in harmony and awareness.
[BELL]

Dwelling in the refuge of Buddha,
I clearly see the path of light and beauty in the world.
Dwelling in the refuge of Dharma,

I learn to open many doors on the path of transformation.
Dwelling in the refuge of Sangha,
shining light that supports me, keeping my practice free of
obstruction.
[BELL]

Taking refuge in the Buddha in myself,
I aspire to help all people recognize their own awakened
nature,
realizing the Mind of Love.
Taking refuge in the Dharma in myself,
I aspire to help all people fully master the ways of practice
and walk together on the path of liberation.
Taking refuge in the Sangha in myself,
I aspire to help all people build Fourfold Communities,
to embrace all beings and support their transformation.
[BELL, BELL]

## 14. Sharing the Merit
Transmitting the trainings, practicing the way of awareness
gives rise to benefits without limit.
We vow to share the fruits with all beings.
We vow to offer tribute to parents, teachers, friends,
and numerous beings
who give guidance and support along the path.
[BELL, BELL, BELL]

## CEREMONY TO RECITE THE THREE REFUGES, TWO PROMISES, AND FIVE MINDFULNESS TRAININGS

[DURING THE FIVE MINDFULNESS TRAININGS RECITATION CEREMONY, THE HEAD OF CEREMONY SHOULD BE SOMEONE WHO IS STABLE IN THE PRACTICE.]

### 1. OPENING THE CEREMONY

*Sitting Meditation* [12 MINUTES]

*Incense Offering*
In gratitude, we offer this incense
throughout space and time
to all Buddhas and Bodhisattvas.
May it be fragrant as Earth herself,
reflecting careful efforts, wholehearted awareness,
and the fruit of understanding slowly ripening.
May we and all beings
be companions of Buddhas and Bodhisattvas.
May we awaken from forgetfulness
and realize our true home.

*Touching the Earth*
*Opening Gatha*
The one who bows and the one who is bowed to
are both, by nature, empty.
Therefore the communication between them
is inexpressibly perfect.

Our practice center is the Net of Indra
reflecting all Buddhas everywhere.
And with my person in front of each Buddha,
I go with my whole life for refuge.
[BELL]

*Prostrations*
[TOUCH THE EARTH AT EACH SOUND OF THE BELL]

Offering light in the Ten Directions,
the Buddha, the Dharma, and the Sangha,
to whom we bow in gratitude.
[BELL]

Teaching and living the way of awareness
in the very midst of suffering and confusion,
Shakyamuni Buddha, the Fully Enlightened One,
to whom we bow in gratitude.
[BELL]

Cutting through ignorance, awakening our hearts and
our minds,
Manjushri, the Bodhisattva of Great Understanding,
to whom we bow in gratitude.
[BELL]

Working mindfully, working joyfully for the sake of
all beings,
Samantabhadra, the Bodhisattva of Great Action,
to whom we bow in gratitude.
[BELL]

Listening deeply, serving beings in countless ways,
Avalokiteshvara, the Bodhisattva of Great Compassion,
to whom we bow in gratitude.
[BELL]

Fearless and persevering through realms of suffering and
darkness,
Kshitigarbha, the Bodhisattva of Great Aspiration,
to whom we bow in gratitude.
[BELL]

Seed of awakening and loving kindness
in children and all beings,
Maitreya, the Buddha to-be-born,
to whom we bow in gratitude.
[BELL]

Showing the way fearlessly and compassionately,
the stream of all our Ancestral Teachers,
to whom we bow in gratitude.
[BELL, BELL]

## 2. OPENING VERSE
[BELL, BELL, BELL]
Namo Tassa Bhagavato Arahato Samma Sambuddhassa
Namo Tassa Bhagavato Arahato Samma Sambuddhassa
Namo Tassa Bhagavato Arahato Samma Sambuddhassa
[BELL]

The Dharma is deep and lovely.
We now have a chance to see, study, and practice it.

We vow to realize its true meaning.

[BELL]

## 3. The Heart of Perfect Understanding

The Bodhisattva Avalokita,
while moving in the deep course of Perfect Understanding,
shed light on the Five Skandhas and found them equally
empty.
After this penetration, he overcame ill-being.

[BELL]

Listen, Shariputra,
form is emptiness, and emptiness is form.
Form is not other than emptiness, emptiness is not other
than form.
The same is true with feelings, perceptions, mental formations, and consciousness.

[BELL]

Listen, Shariputra,
all dharmas are marked with emptiness.
They are neither produced nor destroyed,
neither defiled nor immaculate,
neither increasing nor decreasing.
Therefore in emptiness there is neither form, nor feelings,
nor perceptions, nor mental formations, nor consciousness.
No eye, or ear, or nose, or tongue, or body, or mind.
No form, no sound, no smell, no taste, no touch, no object
of mind.
No realms of elements (from eyes to mind consciousness),

no interdependent origins and no extinction of them
(from ignorance to death and decay).
No ill-being, no cause of ill-being, no end of ill-being, and no
path.
No understanding and no attainment.
[BELL]

Because there is no attainment,
the Bodhisattvas, grounded in Perfect Understanding,
find no obstacles for their minds.
Having no obstacles, they overcome fear,
liberating themselves forever from illusion, realizing perfect
nirvana.
All Buddhas in the past, present, and future,
thanks to this Perfect Understanding,
arrive at full, right, and universal enlightenment.
[BELL]

Therefore one should know
that Perfect Understanding is the highest mantra, the unequaled mantra,
the destroyer of ill-being, the incorruptible truth.
A mantra of Prajñaparamita should therefore be proclaimed:

Gate gate paragate parasamgate bodhi svaha
Gate gate paragate parasamgate bodhi svaha
Gate gate paragate parasamgate bodhi svaha
[BELL, BELL]

## 4. Introductory Words

Today the community has gathered to recite the Three Refuges, the Two Promises, and the Five Mindfulness Trainings. First we will recite the Three Refuges and the Two Promises. Young members of the community, please come forward. Upon hearing the sound of the bell, please touch the Earth three times to show your gratitude to the Buddha, the Dharma, and the Sangha.

[BELL, BELL, BELL]

[YOUNG PEOPLE TOUCH THE EARTH THREE TIMES ]

## 5. The Three Refuges

Young students of the Buddha, you have taken refuge in the Buddha, the one who shows you the way in this life; in the Dharma, the way of understanding and love; and in the Sangha, the community that lives in harmony and awareness. It is beneficial to recite the Three Refuges regularly. Will the entire community please join the young people in reciting after me:

I take refuge in the Buddha,
the one who shows me the way in this life.
[BELL]

I take refuge in the Dharma,
the way of understanding and of love.
[BELL]

I take refuge in the Sangha,
the community that lives in harmony and awareness.
[BELL, BELL]

### 6. THE TWO PROMISES (FOR CHILDREN)

Young students of the Buddha, we have completed the recitation of the Three Refuges. Now we will recite the Two Promises that you have made with the Buddha, the Dharma, and the Sangha. Will the entire community please join the young people in reciting after me:

I vow to develop understanding, in order to live peacefully with people, animals, plants, and minerals.

This is the First Promise you have made with the Buddha, our teacher. Have you tried to learn more about it and to keep your promise during the past two weeks?
[BELL]

I vow to develop my compassion, in order to protect the lives of people, animals, plants, and minerals.

This is the Second Promise you have made with the Buddha, our teacher. Have you tried to learn more about it and to keep your promise during the past two weeks?
[BELL]

Young students of the Enlightened One, understanding and love are the two most important teachings of the Buddha. If we do not make the effort to be open, to understand the suffering of other people, we will not be able to love them and to live in harmony with them. We should also try to understand and protect the lives of animals, plants, and minerals and live in harmony with them. If we cannot understand, we cannot love. The Buddha teaches us to look at living beings with the eyes of love and understanding. Please learn to practice this teaching.

Young people, upon hearing the sound of the bell, please stand up and touch the Earth three times to the Three Jewels.

[BELL, BELL, BELL]

[THE YOUNG PEOPLE TOUCH THE EARTH]

[THE YOUNG PEOPLE MAY NOW LEAVE THE HALL OR THEY MAY STAY TO LISTEN TO THE OTHER TRAININGS. ]

## 7. SANGHAKARMAN PROCEDURE*

Sanghakarman Master: Has the entire community assembled?

Sangha Convener: The entire community has assembled.

Sanghakarman Master: Is there harmony in the community?*

Sangha Convener: Yes, there is harmony.

Sanghakarman Master: Is there anyone not able to be present who has asked to be represented, and have they declared themselves to have done their best to study and practice the Five Mindfulness Trainings?

Sangha Convener: No, there is not.

*or*

Sangha Convener: Yes, [NAME], for health reasons, cannot be at the recitation today. She has asked [NAME] to represent her and she declares that she has done her best to study and practice the mindfulness trainings.

Sanghakarman Master: What is the reason for the community gathering today?

* The recitation of the Five Mindfulness Trainings should be done when the community is in harmony. The practice of Beginning Anew will help the community resolve conflicts.

Sangha Convener: The community has gathered to practice the recitation of the Five Mindfulness Trainings.

Sanghakarman Master: Noble community, please listen. Today, [DATE], has been declared to be the Mindfulness Training Recitation Day. We have gathered at the appointed time. The noble community is ready to hear and recite the mindfulness trainings in an atmosphere of harmony, and the recitation can proceed. Is this statement clear and complete?

Everyone: Clear and complete.

[BELL]

## 8. Introductory Words

Brothers and Sisters, it is now time to recite the Five Mindfulness Trainings.

[OPTIONAL: PLEASE, THOSE WHO HAVE BEEN ORDAINED AS UPASAKA AND UPASIKA KNEEL WITH JOINED PALMS IN THE DIRECTION OF THE BUDDHA, OUR TEACHER.]

Brothers and Sisters, please listen. The Five Mindfulness Trainings are the basis for a happy life. They have the capacity to protect life and to make it beautiful and worth living. They are also the door that opens to enlightenment and liberation. Please listen to each mindfulness training, and answer "yes" silently every time you see that you have made an effort to study, practice, and observe the mindfulness training read.

## 9. Reciting the Five Mindfulness Trainings

*The First Mindfulness Training*

Aware of the suffering caused by the destruction of life, I am committed to cultivating compassion and learning ways to protect the lives of people, animals, plants, and minerals. I am determined not to kill, not to let others kill, and not to support any act of killing in the world, in my thinking, and in my way of life.

This is the first of the Five Mindfulness Trainings. Have you made an effort to study, practice and observe it during the past two weeks?

[THREE BREATHS]

[BELL]*

*The Second Mindfulness Training*

Aware of the suffering caused by exploitation, social injustice, stealing, and oppression, I am committed to cultivating loving kindness and learning ways to work for the well-being of people, animals, plants, and minerals. I will practice generosity by sharing my time, energy, and material resources with those who are in real need. I am determined not to steal and not to possess anything that should belong to others. I will respect the property of others, but I will prevent others from profiting from human suffering or the suffering of other species on Earth.

This is the second of the Five Mindfulness Trainings. Have you made an effort to study, practice and observe it during the past two weeks?

[THREE BREATHS]

[BELL]

---

* After three breaths, the bell master "stops" the bell by holding the striker gently against the rim, thereby signaling the reader to continue with the next mindfulness training.

*The Third Mindfulness Training*
Aware of the suffering caused by sexual misconduct, I am committed to cultivating responsibility and learning ways to protect the safety and integrity of individuals, couples, families, and society. I am determined not to engage in sexual relations without love and a long-term commitment. To preserve the happiness of myself and others, I am determined to respect my commitments and the commitments of others. I will do everything in my power to protect children from sexual abuse and to prevent couples and families from being broken by sexual misconduct.

This is the third of the Five Mindfulness Trainings. Have you made an effort to study, practice and observe it during the past two weeks?

[THREE BREATHS]

[BELL]

*The Fourth Mindfulness Training*
Aware of the suffering caused by unmindful speech and the inability to listen to others, I am committed to cultivating loving speech and deep listening in order to bring joy and happiness to others and relieve others of their suffering. Knowing that words can create happiness or suffering, I am determined to speak truthfully, with words that inspire self-confidence, joy, and hope. I will not spread news that I do not know to be certain and will not criticize or condemn things of which I am not sure. I will refrain from uttering words that can cause division or discord, or that can cause the family or the community to break. I am determined to make all efforts to reconcile and resolve all conflicts, however small.

This is the fourth of the Five Mindfulness Trainings. Have you made an effort to study, practice and observe it during the past two weeks?

[THREE BREATHS]

[BELL]

*The Fifth Mindfulness Training*

Aware of the suffering caused by unmindful consumption, I am committed to cultivating good health, both physical and mental, for myself, my family, and my society by practicing mindful eating, drinking, and consuming. I will ingest only items that preserve peace, well-being, and joy in my body, in my consciousness, and in the collective body and consciousness of my family and society. I am determined not to use alcohol or any other intoxicant or to ingest foods or other items that contain toxins, such as certain TV programs, magazines, books, films, and conversations. I am aware that to damage my body or my consciousness with these poisons is to betray my ancestors, my parents, my society, and future generations. I will work to transform violence, fear, anger, and confusion in myself and in society by practicing a diet for myself and for society. I understand that a proper diet is crucial for self-transformation and for the transformation of society.

This is the fifth of the Five Mindfulness Trainings. Have you made an effort to study, practice and observe it during the past two weeks?

[THREE BREATHS]

[BELL]

## 10. CONCLUDING WORDS

Brothers and Sisters, we have recited the Five Mindfulness Trainings, the foundation of happiness for the individual, the family, and society. We should recite them regularly so that our study and practice of the mindfulness trainings can deepen day by day.

Upon hearing the sound of the bell, please stand up and touch the Earth three times to show your gratitude to the Buddha, the Dharma, and the Sangha.

[BELL, BELL, BELL]

## 11. THE THREE REFUGES

I take refuge in the Buddha,
the one who shows me the way in this life.
I take refuge in the Dharma,
the way of understanding and of love.
I take refuge in the Sangha,
the community that lives in harmony and awareness.

[BELL]

Dwelling in the refuge of Buddha,
I clearly see the path of light and beauty in the world.
Dwelling in the refuge of Dharma,
I learn to open many doors on the path of transformation.
Dwelling in the refuge of Sangha,
shining light that supports me, keeping my practice free of obstruction.

[BELL]

Taking refuge in the Buddha in myself,
I aspire to help all people recognize their own awakened nature,

realizing the Mind of Love.
Taking refuge in the Dharma in myself,
I aspire to help all people fully master the ways of practice
and walk together on the path of liberation.
Taking refuge in the Sangha in myself,
I aspire to help all people build Fourfold Communities,
to embrace all beings and support their transformation.
[BELL, BELL]

## 12. Sharing the Merit

Reciting the trainings, practicing the way of awareness
gives rise to benefits without limit.
We vow to share the fruits with all beings.
We vow to offer tribute to parents, teachers, friends, and numerous beings
who give guidance and support along the path.
[BELL, BELL, BELL]

Parallax Press, a nonprofit organization, publishes books on engaged Buddhism and the practice of mindfulness by Thich Nhat Hanh and other authors. All of Thich Nhat Hanh's work is available at our online store and in our free catalog. For a copy of the catalog, please contact:

Parallax Press
**www.parallax.org**
P.O. Box 7355
Berkeley, CA 94707
Tel: (510) 525-0101

Individuals, couples, and families are invited to practice the art of mindful living in the tradition of Thich Nhat Hanh at retreat communities in France and the United States. For information, please visit www.plumvillage.org or contact:

Plum Village
13 Martineau
33580 Dieulivol, France
info@plumvillage.org

Green Mountain Dharma Center
P.O. Box 182
Hartland Four Corners, VT 05049
mfmaster@vermontel.net
Tel: (802) 436-1103

Deer Park Monastery
2499 Melru Lane
Escondido, CA 92026
deerpark@plumvillage.org
Tel: (760) 291-1003

For a worldwide directory of Sanghas practicing in the tradition of Thich Nhat Hanh, please visit www.iamhome.org